Michael Frederick

SHY ANN

A Novel by
Michael Frederick

Dedicated to my brother John

Novels by author:
"WHITE SHOULDERS"
"LEDGES"
"THE PAPER MAN"
"MISSOURI MADNESS"

May, 2002/1st printing

Dwayne

I am a writer. My name is Dwayne Dayne. Don't laugh.
My father picked my name when I was finally delivered at 8:52
A.M. in the Methodist Hospital in Woodbury, Iowa, the biggest
city in Western Iowa. My mother was out of it after my delivery,
sedated heavily, long before forceps and several stitches. I was her
first child and most difficult birth of three, two boys and a girl.

My middle name is Harvey, my father's surname. Since I'm
a writer, I use D. H. Dayne as my pen name. Sounds better. I
don't blame my old man for giving me such a silly sounding name, a
name that helped me believe early on that kids are cruel.

A service buddy of my dad's was named Dwayne. They
went into the service together just before WWII when they were
18. His service buddy Dwayne was from Wayne, Nebraska.
Dwayne from Wayne was the guy my dad had the most fun with
while in the service. My dad laughed hard every time he talked
about his buddy. He said they had more fun together, dancing in
clubs, chasing women, and using Dwayne from Wayne as a great
icebreaker to meet women. My dad would smile so big when he
would tell me how he and his buddy would approach two girls
sitting together; my dad would be behind Dwayne, ready to ask the
other girl to dance when both girls were laughing from Dwayne's
introduction:

—Hi! I'm Dwayne from Wayne!

It was Dwayne from Wayne, the right sound and a smile
with a sense of play, that gave him his light and many dances. I've
never had that sense of play...until now. Not because of my name.
I use D. H. Dayne on my book covers, and, like Dwayne from
Wayne, I've had fun with my name and accept it, and honor my
beloved father by using it.

One Good Reader

It's the kind of story, or incident in a story I've always wanted to write about. Or rather, it's this small-town mood this incident stirs inside me that I want to capture. If I could only get the damn thing...I mean...blessed thing out of me, get it into my brain long enough to push it down, through my heart, and move it along to my left hand (my writing hand), and scrawl it out before it's lost forever. You will then know this essence I'm feeling, in 1st or 3rd person, because I am not a writer/in.

No man or woman, including politicians or preachers or even traveling salesmen, has worked and walked, observed and talked in the small towns of America as much as I have. I can say this because it's true, though most of that time in my youth my awareness bordered on unconsciousness.

The incident I'm talking about is unusual. It just happened last September, about a month ago, in the midst of all this terrorist insanity.

I've always been a writer, a self-published writer. Some dismiss me as a real writer because I self publish. I understand tha and I hate that. The rejection letters on my wall prove it.

My sister Karen is a librarian in Phoenix.   She called me or my 800 number (of course) to tell me about this incident related to my novel *Ledges*. To appreciate the effect this incident has, I must set it up with a bit of explanation:

My father died in May of '96. I know his death caused me to write more and more. His death changed me a thousand ways emotionally, one of which made me a better writer. So many writers have said so much more than I ever could about the death of a loved one. All I know is that his death was the second of thre men very close to me. The first man you all know as John Candy

actor. I knew John only through my fictional character Wayne
ny original screenplay titled *Wayne*. I will cover this later.

Soon after my father dies, I moved to Asheville, North
rolina to heal. I did, somewhat. Then, with a modest
eritance, I took a gamble and opened a telemarketing service for
ropractors in Marietta, Georgia near Life Chiropractic College
h Life students working for me. It failed. I lost my shirt under
unbearable sound of speeding freight trains that constantly
nbled and roared through downtown Marietta.

I moved to Tallahassee, Florida, nearly broke (on many
els); I went there to live near my daughter who was in high
ool then. I lived in an apartment across the street from Lake
a, walking around it many times a day with this story *Ledges* on
mind. This story was a respite from my failure in Marietta. My
am had crashed. I wanted to make a fortune and take one of my
ries (screenplays) straight-to-video. Not.

In Florida, I wrote every day, not knowing where *Ledges*
s going, though I knew I was onto something good because I
d the spine of a script, *the Spanking*, I was using as a guide to
ry-line.

This feeling of having something with *Ledges* told me I had
go to Ledges State Park in Central Iowa where the story takes
ce. I had been to Ledges briefly with a girlfriend from
arshalltown, Iowa; the place really made an impression on me.

Pulling a U-Haul all the way to Boone, Iowa (the town
arest to Ledges), I had most of the story written except I had to
to Ledges and capture that place on paper, the essence of it. I
ve straight through from Florida, smoking a pack of cigarettes
ery 500 miles. Deep down, what bothered me the most: I knew I
uld never find a publisher who would like my work enough to
blish it. My writing would be laughed into the slush pile, and I
uld never be a writer/in.

It was springtime in Ledges when I parked my car and U-

Haul in a parking area near the back entrance to Iowa's oldest state park. I walked with my notebook riding my hip along nature trails lined with trail side data that kept me writing every fifty feet or so.

Ledges was an incredible space of protected nature I had all to myself that day. I knew I had discovered the perfect place for my book to take place, but I could not wait for some publisher to discover it, too. That would most possibly never happen. So, with my extensive business-to-business telemarketing experience...I managed to borrow just enough money to get *Ledges* printed, right off my typewriter. The printer had to shrink my text in order to hit the page count, in order to keep my price down. It's always about money.

I was in my mid-40's when I hit the bricks with 5,000 copies of *Ledges* (my second novel) stacked in my rented garage in Woodbury, Iowa, the town in which I had spent most of my youth.

It took as much courage as stupidity to sell a self-published novel door-to-door to businesses in that neck of the woods. After my first calls on grocery stores, bookstores, drugstores, florists, gift shops, and beauty shops in Northwest Iowa small towns, I realized I was ugly. Instead of genuine smiling faces from prospects, or even courtesy smiles because of my youth, my once handsome face was now tense and soured by the fact I was doing this at 45 instead of 27, hawking my self-published novel for 4 bucks a copy, 48 dollars a dozen, right in the middle of "Hicksville," my old stomping grounds, in America's Heartland...again.

Twenty years ago I was a successful paper man (toilet paper salesman) in this area known as the tri-state area. I knew you "can't go home again," but I always wanted to experience that feeling of returning home and seeing that things are *not* the same.

A big part of returning home for me was returning to the small towns in Iowa, Nebraska, and South Dakota; returning to sell a product like *Ledges*, a four-dollar item I could sell the piss out of. It had to be sold in this place of heartache where I lost my father.

dges was written from my heart and had to be sold first near dges where the heart of the story takes place. Ames and Boone uld be my targets.

I did need easy sales, because I knew that if an ugly writer n get easy money, into that green river of prosperity and give out s feeling he is making people happy along his way, he can and ll begin to re-youth, by smiling and laughing most of the day. All cause he believes he is closing in on his dream to be a writer/in.

He will sell his book to surprised motel clerks in little towns d get four bucks knocked off his thirty-dollar room. He will not e at the end of the day when he counts his money from his ndleless sales case that carried a dozen books at a time.

He will get up early in the morning, on tender feet and uised shins, and cuss all the way through his shower and the ading of his stuff into his father's car. Each time: it will remind m that his father is not here to see him in the territory.

Within ten minutes, a surprised waitress in a café will buy e book that pays for his breakfast. This is the space of time when writes a bit, picking up where he left off in his story. He will ay away from newspapers and television in order to get back to here he was: lost—lost in his story before the brutal day in the nches begins.

When businesses are just opening, he walks Main Street, ually the town's square, his eyes sweeping every storefront for ospects; hopefully, they are not too busy to listen. Though he is sted, he is ugly until he breaks the ice. That's why he must sell to s first prospect—even if it's one book for some friend or relative the prospect, someone who enjoys pleasure reading.

This is the time he is glad that he wrote just a little, earlier in e café, when he was rested. Now, he looks forward to lunch after good sales morning. Then, he can write a bit more while left one in a crowded café, moving his next book along—one thought, e sentence at a time. Between his words, he knows deep down he is still a better salesman than writer, all because he's had to spend twenty times the energy and time, six days a week, selling hi books to strangers.

All morning he will surprise his prospects, for never have they been pitched by a self-published novelist trying to sell his book. He will have averaged a dozen books sold per hour, unless he's in close proximity to where his story takes place; if so: it will be double that or better. And with these good numbers, he will relax more, and smile more. All because of the money riding his hi inside his sales case is too much to remember now. He has been validated as a working man, and soon will have some readers who think he is not ugly at all. For now, men admire him; women buy his books because of this effulgence he has. Yet, somewhere in the writer's pink brain matter, in the abstruse recesses of the brain that can command the heart to feel joy—in that speck of space reserved for everlasting glory, confidence and constant celebration—he knows: he is not a writer/in. He knows he is not a published writer validated by that powerful loop of editors, agents, and publishers who tell us all who is good enough to be in print.

If a self-published writer can sell two dozen books at a time to a grocery chain—three, four, sometimes more in a day—he will skip lunch and refuel when he's landed, because hunger is in the mind for this kind of writer, perhaps near that same speck in the brain that touches the will to be a writer/in.

He will make calls until his prospects go home. He will do this Monday through Saturday and find it hard to rest on Sunday. And when he's sold his heart and soul in all kinds of weather for those books to be sold to readers, he will cuss again when his books are returned to him demanding a refund.

This madness went on from September to March for D. H. Dayne. A fan letter here and there kept him optimistic while returned books for refunds kept coming in; he was getting more and more burnt out.

Then, Dwayne's body began to tell him: it isn't working.
 had to check into a Woodbury hospital for exhaustion, getting
 IV for dehydration.

Two weeks later, paranoid because of his father's wrongful
ath after bypass surgery 18 months ago, Dwayne thought he was
ving a heart attack. He checked himself into an Omaha out-
tients' hospital. Three hours and five hundred bucks later: he
s driving home for Woodbury, up I-29 after his second IV in two
eks.

I knew it was coming, just as downtown Woodbury was
ming into view—I had to run south to Phoenix and move in with
 brother and parents in my brother's Tempe condo. The money
ad borrowed to get my book printed was due to be paid back. I
s in debt up to my ears after selling three thousand *Ledges* in five
onths...the hard way. I had used the money I saved from book
les to order another five thousand copies of *Ledges*; I did this
fore the refunds were coming in steady, because things looked
omising. And, I literally swore I'd never work another frigin'
ad-end job, and from now on, be a writer and live off my
iting...or die.

Phoenix was my big struggle in so many ways; I wished
any times I had never gone there, though I discovered my only
ssible market while there: public libraries.

I will skip my Phoenix struggle; a self-published writer can
 that, because...who cares?

Anyway, my sister Karen the librarian, moved to Phoenix
th me. She gave me the idea to telemarket to libraries. Karen is
ndicapped, physically—not mentally, that's for sure. She
ipped) off a cliff at White Eagle's grave in Woodbury, rolling
me two hundred feet to the bottom, severely injuring discs all
ong her spine. Karen didn't get care for her injuries. Over time,
e became a fused tuna. I called her Ironsides when she first got
r wheelchair. She got back at me by having me push her all over

Phoenix in 110° heat. She thought that was funny. I guess because she's had the personality of my character Pam in *Ledges*. I've always told her that the comedienne Roseanne looks a lot like her.

When I moved to Asheville, North Carolina about a year later, I had managed to place my first two (claimed) novels in about three thousand public libraries by selling them one at a time. My second novel (that I claim) *The Paper Man*, I had printed in Phoenix. Then, for the first time, with two books to sell at one time, I began to make money. The best part: *Ledges*, with its small print and all of its flaws, was circulating well in over 80% of my libraries. Thank God.

Criticism kept coming in from readers and librarians. Karen now gets all of my mail and email. I put her phone number and addresses on my books, because she's stable and I'm not. One such feedback came with a check. It read: "Mr. Dayne, for heaven's sake, get a decent editor! Your ideas may be worth telling, but I was so distracted by the sloppy construction I couldn't finish the book. Didn't get past the first two chapters, in fact. Keep writing, but get some help."

Karen keeps track of my library circulations. I update her every week on my new libraries. She knows where my "hot" libraries are, that is, where my books circulate well. See, Karen's a pro on a computer, and she's smart.

That's what brings me to this incident I'm talking about—the one I always wanted to write about. As I lay here in my bed in October 2001, in my rented Oteen cabin outside of Asheville in the foothills of the Blue Ridge Mountains, with my country at war against terrorism, I got a call from Karen today. She told me about this town named Grey in Maine. The Grey librarian had been e-mailing other Maine librarians about the incident:

Apparently, Grey's oldest resident was in her 90's when she died at home while reading in her favorite chair last winter. Yes, it was my book *Ledges* she was reading in her favorite chair when she

-8-

t this world to meet her Maker. The librarian had heard this from
e daughter of the deceased patron who went to check on her
other.

The Grey librarian told my sister that the old lady was a
racious reader with a terrific memory and a magnifier. The
hole town knew she loved to read books and was never overdue.
 fact, Grey's oldest library patron always talked about how a
od book was her greatest joy, and that she was Grey's most
olific reader, year after year.

Now: all 457 Grey residents want to read this book *Ledges*
cause their oldest resident dropped dead while reading it. They
 wanted to see for themselves if this story *Ledges* has something
ecial about it that made the old lady croak.

Of course, Karen, with her dry sense of humor, milked this
rey incident in order to alarm her sensitive brother, telling him on
e phone today:

—Gee, Dwayne, just think...thanks to *Ledges* you have one
ss reader in Maine.

—Real funny, Karen. I s'pose you got the librarian sayin'
y book killed my reader. Did you say that, Karen?

(I hated her laugh because it made me laugh.) Then, when
e had tortured her brother long enough:

—No, Dwayne...I said it's a strange thing to happen. She
id she had to die reading something, because she read all the time.
ne said she would love to have you come to her library for a book
gning. Your books are hot there, brother.

—Maine's too far from me, Karen. I told you to set me up
ith libraries that are close together or the gas will eat me alive!

—Relax, Dwayne. I can't set you up till you're ready. Did
innebago get back to you?

—Yeah, I'm real close to buyin' a new one. It's a big step,
aren.

—I know. I'll keep taking your calls and mail and

depositing your checks...but I want a hundred a week if I schedule your book signings.

—We'll see how it goes. I don't want you to run me around on this astrology chart yer doin'. After a month or so we'll know how it's goin' for both of us. You know I'll be fair with ya, Karen.

—Yeah, Karen laughed.

That was the incident: the death of a stranger, a reader in Maine. I imagined what it would be like to go up to that little town in Maine, now, in October. How typical it is in America, for a death to bring life and demand for a writer's work. Even if I am a celebrity of sorts in Grey, Maine..I'm still not a writer/in.

He imagined the good food and fresh coffee the town would have for him in their only café on the square. And if any single women were left in Grey, he would be the reason they dressed up—to go to his book signing in their little brownstone library on Main Street, next to the fire station across from Mary's one-station beauty shop and catty corner from the A & P that was next to the drugstore that, every month, had supplied his dead reader with four different medications for her bad heart; and those plastic bottles with her name typed on them, standing right next to her, at her side on the tray right next to her favorite reading chair.

I suppose strong emotions can kill, if felt deeply enough in a story, but unresolved trauma can't be found in an autopsy or proven to be culpable. Even though the little pills from the local drugstore will certainly show up in my reader's system, the whole town agrees that it was the little pills that kept the old lady alive all these years; besides, her prescription is a far cry from a deliberate act, not like that self-published writer who did such a perfidious deed by writing that damn story her daughter found in her cold hands on top of her lifeless bosom, the last two pages of the open ook flat on her heart.

      Yes, this writer's imagination always wanted to begin a
ory like this, and keep "the incident" growing when he finds out
om the Grey librarian who bought the book from him, that the
hole damn town wants to read D. H. Dayne's book. "A
uriosity," the librarian called it, adding her haughty, lilting laugh
at annoyed this now-famous writer in Grey, Maine. A writer who
lways wanted to be a writer/in.

Balls of Rejection

Long, long into the night I lay awake in my Asheville cabin, with the first breeze of October chilling my dark bedroom. I was thinking about how I should tell this story, i.e., in what tense; and I was recalling the day I found out John Candy had died.

As a self-published writer, I want to use both 1st and 3rd person. And so: he did. Only a self-published writer dares to do such a terrible thing that's so bold and yet so confusing and annoying to his readers. Some of them will understand this and finish my books. Those of you who drop me and say, "forget this guy," will go away and never return to me. You will be the ones who validate why I am not a writer/in, a published writer accepted into the loop of writers published the conventional way: get an agent, who finds a publisher, who prints your book, and then gets a distributor to market it.

To all of you who drop me and return my work unread: DROP DEAD! I will continue to write and publish my books without your help. And know that I will continue to do better than most writers, because most writers are not published at all.

I know my readers better than most writers. They are not very educated, with degrees on the wall or in the homogenous follow-the-herd sense of getting a college degree. My readers are mostly women, all ages; they are people who want to get lost in my stories. But, just as many, or even more, leave me before they finish any of my books.

I thank God I have a following. In three and a half years I have managed to sell enough books to public libraries, independent bookstores, and gift shops to get over five hundred thousand readers, in every state but Hawaii (at this time). And my books really do circulate well in Canada. That is why I'm making the

ggest move and purchase of my life. Thanks to my readers, I'm
lying my first home, and furniture, too. Now I'll be able to live
nywhere I choose, all because of them, my precious readers who
upport this dream of mine to become a writer/in.

And soon I will live among them, in their towns and parks in
ly Winnebago Adventurer motor home. I will live everywhere yet
owhere, and continue writing as long as they keep reading my
ork. As for the rest of you who dis me: go to hell.

My readers have given me the courage to tell 'em all to go
o hell. And they support my changing tenses; they put up with my
un-on sentences and a thousand other mistakes glaring at them in
very chapter I write.

His name is D. H. Dayne. He moved from his side onto his
ack, under his open bedroom window in his cracker box rental
abin nestled in the Caroline Pines in Oteen, North Carolina in east
sheville.

Again, he was thinking how he lost three important men in
is life as October was now here. He could feel his heart thumping
lood in his wrists and feet, pulling at him to get up and meet these
rst glorious minutes of the second October in the new century.

He got out of bed and dressed in the dark room lit only by a
arolina harvest moon that was vanilla colored and as big as a
umpkin hanging directly over his cabin. The only other light: the
umbers on his clock radio that read 12:04 as he pulled on his blue
weatshirt with its silver wolf in snow stenciled on the front. He
ut his face close to his dresser mirror in the moonlight just to see if
e could see any light coming from his weak blue eyes. None.

Then: he kept his face close to the mirror, moving it over to
ne taped black and white photo of Thomas Wolfe, Asheville's most
amous writer, that was eye level on the mirror if sitting down.
ayne squinted at Tom's brown eyes that had a feverish glow then,

especially in October. Thomas Wolfe is the only reason Dwayne Harvey Dayne is in Asheville. Dwayne's favorite writer's numinous spirit, this October, will be the catalyst for his most important move, and his next novel.

Dwayne went into his small front room and picked up his walking shoes off yesterday's newspaper. As he sat in the dark on his furnished half-sofa, putting on his shoes, he felt confined like in a cage, no, a bird cage, and he laughed out loud. He hustled out his back door after grabbing his glasses off his dresser.

In the moonlight: there was Lawn Boy, his 4-cylinder blue Hyundai, parked close to the cabin back door. He patted Lawn Boy's trunk as he crunched away on his gravel drive that led uphill.

He was thinking about his name, and how he uses D. H. Dayne on his books because if Dwayne Dayne is repeated fast enough, it sounds like a knucklehead—a crazy person's name. Since October was Dwayne's month of change, he was thinking of changing his pen name on his 4th novel, but couldn't because his 3rd novel was circulating so well in libraries, and helping his first two books go off the shelf. And, because of his 3rd book: he was making this big move into a motor home.

The sounds of children laughing, as they mockingly repeated Dwayne Dayne in grade school, could still make him blush, even now in his late 40's.

Carolina Pines are alive in the winds channeled through the frosty Blue Ridge Mountains surrounding him. This walk, late at night, uphill mostly, follows a circuitous path he can follow from memory without moonlight. His feet are light and recognized by chained dogs along his route. Even at night, they will not bark at him, for they know him and whine for him to stop and talk to them softly as he does every time he passes by.

He could think and reminisce now as no other time of day. He was thinking of his unclaimed first novel as he walked the rutted tire trail that curved north for a quarter-mile. To himself:

—I was a better salesman than a writer then, he chuckled.

I thought about how I have a sales record for a self-published writer that will always be untouchable; in fact, I knew no other writer has attempted to break it, because certain insanity or dementia would stop him. I use"him" because I know that no woman is dumb enough or bull-headed enough to do exactly what I did for two years.

In 100 weeks, Dwayne Harvey Dayne personally sold ten thousand copies of his unclaimed first novel. He sold 20 copies a day at five bucks a copy over some five hundred days; one copy at a time, mostly, to businesses and residents, door to door.

The double tire trail was easy to see; he stayed on the left one from habit as he passed the old rooftop ballroom he knew Thomas Wolfe had been to in 1937 during his last visit home with just over a year of his life remaining.

Behind the car wash, Dwayne turned right onto a dark residential road that dead-ended after a mile and turned to dirt for another mile. That old rhythm of the moon's rays bathed him in this invisible sea of uncertainty that scared him enough to know that this uncertainty is exactly why he must make this change in his life.

—My readers will protect me. A half-million readers in three and a half years. A half-million.

October moons had this effect on him since boyhood. He noticed it more and more in his 40's with every new autumn. That's why his sister's sidereal locator chart appealed to him. He knew some things connected him to the stars, something that was as inexplicable as our eternal question: Why are we here?

Most of his life, Dwayne Dayne believed in the omnipotent, bearded god, who sent His only Son here to be tortured and martyred—so we could live. But now: he was searching, to the stars, up there; and, perhaps there was something to Karen's chart. He liked the idea of it anyway. Sounded fun.

Yes, glorious October is here!, he wanted to yell. But he kept it in...he kept it inside...until some librarian or retailer wasted his time on the phone and turned him down after leading him on. Then: his fist (the right one) would find a door; his fax machine might be smashed to pieces on the floor because the paper jammed; his chair might get flattened when he bounced it off the floor six or seven times; or his garbage can, stowed under the sink, might break a window.

But not now: for this is my glorious October, my breast-beating king of all seasons is here again.

—This is the month I will begin to manifest my dreams, he smiled.

Till he reached the end of the road, he thought about his herculean book-selling days, doubting if any writer had even sold ten thousand copies in a lifetime of sitting at book signings. His self-talk continued as if he wasn't sure it would interest his readers:

—I was in my roaring twenties. So I had the energy and stupidity to do such a thing. That two years was my college education. I certainly got my masters in sales, that's for sure.

No degree was bestowed on Dwayne when he sold his 10,000th book to a beauty shop receptionist in Denver. There was no fanfare or applause, only a strange look from that receptionist who could see the writer's left hand trembling when his last book was signed and handed to her.

Outside that Denver beauty shop, Dwayne sat down on the curb and cried like a tattered and beaten rebel who had fought a long two-year campaign for and with Robert E. Lee. That day was Dayne's Appomattox. He had surrendered his cause after winning many battles in Arizona, California, New Mexico, Kansas, Colorado, Iowa, Nebraska, and Minnesota, and a few other states where he sold some copies of his first book, his unclaimed novel *White Shoulders*.

His cause was to be a writer/in, a writer discovered then

brought into the publishing loop. With ten thousand readers at the very least, surely, he believed, he'd get "one good reader" who would take him into the fold, into the stable of writers who are really published. Didn't happen.

He left Denver in Rusty, his gold-colored, rusted out 1960 Oldsmobile. Dwayne was nearly broke after spending two hundred bucks on a thick Kodak coupon book he could sell to camera buffs for twenty bucks a coupon that was worth one hundred rolls of Kodak film when redeemed. He had to have some product to sell, and wasn't the least bit afraid of the fact he had no money. But he was afraid of his future, for his back-up plan: to be discovered by a company while on his blistering door-to-door campaign. Again: it didn't happen for him.

When he hit Nebraska, it was early January and it got really cold; so cold that when he closed Rusty's door after getting out, his side-view mirror came unglued and shattered on Lincoln pavement. For the longest time, he stared at Rusty's makeshift radio antenna, a coat hanger that waved in the 30-below wind chill.

He would sell a coupon here and there in little Nebraska towns, going into mostly modern one-story high schools where a camera geek would pop for his Kodak deal with more cash in his pocket than Dwayne had to his name. He thought: How can I return as such a loser to my hometown?

His beard wasn't gray then, but he looked old and beaten down like the heels on his shoes that were now worn flat, like bowler's shoes, from three thousand miles of marching door to door. His once-full, spiked ash blonde hair was now thin and dry and itched all day under a wool rolled-up ski mask. His clear eyes and smiling face—that had sold half his books for him—was gone; he'd turned into the likes of a desperate drifter, a hobo who might not live to see his next meal. But the good people of Nebraska got him home after four out of five shivering nights in Motel 4 (Rusty).

That one good day, he managed to get a fleabag motel.

After a hot bath, he went to this small-town bar and got lucky...or something like that. He met this two hundred-pound farm girl that was built like a haystack with legs. She must've looked good to him, since he looked like an escapee from death row. He laughed at the memory of being bounced on that mushy mattress, his haggard body bent into a horseshoe.

A week later: Dwayne left Woodbury, after hugging Karen goodbye in her crowded but warm little apartment. Her floor was better than Rusty, and some motel mattresses. He drove south, for warmth, and, to hit bottom; leaving his hometown he was relieved he didn't run into any old friends who might see his struggle and failure to be a "real" writer.

It wasn't warm in Texas. In Austin, he had to retire, again, using Rusty's donut spare on his left front wheel. Rusty's sunken left side gave Dwayne the creeps, for with only Rusty's right headlight working, it gave him the sensation of leaning left into the darkness of the centerline.

Yes, he left his hometown broke, with no coupons and an unopened letter his sister gave him announcing his ten-year high school class reunion. He had to do something...or die. His pride had even turned down a twenty-dollar gift his dad offered him. Pride. Pride kills. It really does.

John Candy was alive then. I had been thinking about John playing my character Wayne in my screenplay *Wayne*. Except for John's family and friends, I thought about him as much as anyone before and after he died, I'm sure.

It's funnier if you imagine John Candy doing the things on the next few pages. It wasn't funny at the time, believe me, but it's true; and I don't know if my readers will think it's funny or real or tripe.

The movie *Wayne* begins with John Candy as Wayne

Drummond, 38 years old, homeless, living in his 20-year-old car (Rusty). After leaving his hometown a loser, getting his twenty-year high school reunion letter (unopened) from his sister, he heads south in the cold winter with no money, food, gas, or energy. Wayne flashes back to ten years ago when he was selling his first novel *White Shoulders* door to door in a younger Rusty:

It was the day he sold his personal best of 71 books in one day in Liberal, Kansas. Like a conquering hero, he was auto-graphing books left and right with cash literally stuffed into all his pockets. Back to the present:

Wayne talks to Rusty:

—Now, all I have is a pile of rags on the back seat and an empty gas can on the floor. We sold ten thousand books, called on fifty thousand prospects, and now...huh...nothin'.

Wayne reaches down and opens Rusty's full ashtray; he selects a cigarette butt and lights it with Rusty's lighter that somehow he didn't even push in.

—Thank you, Wayne chuckles to Rusty. Just get me to the next exit. You know the routine.

Later: At a pop machine, he uses a scam he used in his novel *The Paper Man*. He fakes putting change into the soda machine and would get a refund from the motel clerk, usually fifty cents or a buck, just enough to get him to the next business exit. Never would this low scam get him a big meal or a motel.

Anyway, south of Austin: after Wayne gets kicked out of a Motel 6 indoor stairwell for sleeping under it, he tries to make a buck from the motel clerk across the road. Wayne tells her he lost four quarters in her pop machine. To Wayne's surprise, the young clerk is in a wheelchair, very sweet and angelic in appearance. Remember: picture John Candy behind the paralyzed girl, her atrophied legs bent in different directions. He watches her open the pop machine door with a key. After she moves her chair to the side in order to open the wide door, she finds an empty coin box. When she looks up at Wayne with those sad eyes, he swallows hard and says:

—I'm sorry.

When he exited the motel, vowing to himself to never do that again, he meant it.

He and Rusty made it all the way down to Brownsville, Texas around sundown. The only thing Wayne had to eat within the last 48 hours was a Mexican cucumber he bought with his last dime at a roadside vegetable stand near where Rusty had run out of gas.

Wayne, so tired from his drive to get here, had saved the ends of the cucumber and secured them over his eyeballs with a bandana because he had heard that placing cucumbers over the eyes is relaxing.

Dwayne's rumination stopped; he would have to pick up the story later, perhaps on his walk back, for he had reached the end of the dirt road that was tucked back into an open field that overlooked the Blue Ridge foothills. There it was, a hundred yards away. Only a yellow lightbulb burned above the front door of an uninhabited cabin stained brown with some cream-colored stain between the logs.

This is the place where his favorite writer, Thomas Wolfe, came to write, during his last visit home. He came here to get away from the many distractions: family, friends, well-wishers, glad-handing vultures, and more relatives and girls who came down out of the hills to gawk at Asheville's favorite son.

Dwayne only wanted to touch the door handle of the cabin's front door; after that, he pressed his nose to the front window and could see the fireplace mantle Tom leaned on when he had his picture taken over sixty-five years ago.

On Dwayne's trek back home, his thought patterns changed

n the Carolina moonlight. Wayne's story would have to wait. He
ad forty-eight hours to go before his life changed dramatically,
unless tomorrow's mail brings good news.

—They won't even read it, Dwayne scoffed out loud.

His steps on the dirt were soundless below the now-howling
wind and a freight train shunting down by the river that Tom would
ave heard with his whole being. The train's grinding squeal of
metal was a force that could be heard ten miles away at this time of
ight. It was this squealing sound, perhaps the only sound, that can
ake him back to that time and place that defines every writer of the
American novel. For it is the night when that creative feminine past
of our lives can be called forth. This he had learned in Asheville, a
metaphysical place where such things are accepted, a given.

He was Dwayne Dayne then, in his roaring 20's, in the late
70's, living in San Diego. His first novel was written. For twenty
years he never talked about or even claimed his first novel, refusing
even to utter its title to his mind, for it nearly killed him and finished
him off as a writer.

White Shoulders began in the 50's, in January, in Omaha's
massive railroad yard near downtown. A young prostitute cries in
her pimp's car while she holds her newborn baby boy, wrapped in a
blanket. Only the mother's wailing can be heard after the pimp
snatches the baby from its mother and puts the infant inside a
boxcar.

Late into the night, the boxcar moves on the rails across the
desolate countryside of Western Nebraska until...there is a
derailment.

A farmer, in the middle of nowhere, goes to the crash site
and hears a baby's cry above a hissing tanker car that's derailed
next to the same boxcar.

Some twenty years later: Federal Systems Inspector Barney
Cole is at his retirement party in Kansas City when another agent

asks him what ever happened to that baby boy he found at the derailment in Nebraska twenty years ago. Barney didn't know. And that bothered him.

While Barney drives his car through Kansas on his way to retire in New Mexico, he thinks back to that morning when he found the abandoned baby boy alive in the farmer's house. But the farmer was dead, from inhaling toxic fumes of leaking missile fuel from a derailed tanker at the crash site.

Cole remembered the baby was sent to a Topeka orphanage so, he takes a side trip to Topeka and discovers at the orphanage the boy was named Leonard Duncan, illegally adopted by a couple in Hixson, Kansas.

On to Hixson, where Cole finds the 20-year-old Leonard in jail for assaulting his parents. It didn't take the no-nonsense Cole long to determine if Leonard's stammering and twitching face was from the derailment in Nebraska or the Duncan's abuse.

Soon, Leonard was free to ride along with Barney to start a new life.

—To start a new life, Dwayne said out loud when he reached his cabin door, telling himself he'll go to bed now and finish thinking about these things some other time.

—They would always be there. Always, he mumbled, knowing he sometimes talked to himself out loud, a habit from living alone so many years.

—All my characters are a bit like me. Why else write? A man who lives alone must write about himself...or die from ignorance and loneliness.

He looked back at Lawn Boy before going inside, and stared at the moon overhead while thinking about how his looks turned to mediocrity when he hit his 40's. Assiduously he could summon his imagination and could see more than most men that way, though physically his eyes were weak, unattractive and small,

nd pretty much useless without his glasses. He was like his
character Ben in his novel *Ledges*. He knew he named Ben after
Tom's brother Ben. Dwayne asked the moon, silently, if he was
iving alone in middle age because of the maturity he chose as a
oy. He knew Tom would have lived alone in his middle years if he
adn't burned out in his late 30's. He was sure of that.

And Dwayne Dayne, the introverted child and eldest sibling,
ecame the extroverted salesman in the 70's, his roaring 70's.
loyd, his driven paper salesman in his novel *The Paper Man*, was
wayne Dayne in the 70's. Ten thousand towns Dwayne prowled
n the Heartland, selling things, door to door, to businesses—all
lone. That isolation as a salesman on the road gave him the
hance to write, avoiding bars and dependent relationships. It was
un. It was hard.

—I'm tired, he whispered, patting Lawn Boy goodnight.

He went inside knowing that after sleep, he will still be an
nrecognized writer, though half a million readers have gone to bed
onight knowing him. As he took off his shoes in the dark, he
eared his writing would be discovered after he was dead, a f- - -
- - from the publishing world and film industry, who would hear
f his death and want to publish his novels and make his movies. In
nother day or two, he will die, his way of life will die, and he will
ecreate himself.

—After the mail comes, he mumbled, then fell into his bed
nder the open window on the cool sheets from the October air that
vould lift him out of this life soon...so very soon.

She put the book down, on the floor, next to her candle
older. She had read the book from beginning to end in just five
ours. After she blew out her candle, the room smelled of strong/
weet cinnamon, enveloping her floor mattress. She inhaled deeply
e wafting cinnamon fumes that circled and hung in the air so close

to her in the dark studio apartment on Haywood Street, three blocks north of downtown Asheville.

So many have told her it is so rare for a 23-year-old girl, who's so young and attractive, to move clear across the country, alone, without one single friend around to support her. Not a soul really knew her in Asheville, except her co-workers at her two jobs.

But they really don't know her either. She never let anyone really know her. Not yet.

The sound of freight cars shunting down by the French Broad River in the valley to the west was like a lonesome call from the man who became her favorite writer, just because someone she met only once had checked out all his books at the main Asheville Public Library downtown where she worked.

Sleep usually came easy for Ann Bruin, but not tonight. Ann got out of bed in her Bugs Bunny cotton pajamas her mother gave her last Christmas in Portland. She opened her bedroom window just because it had turned to October, her most favorite month of the year, especially after reading his novels and short stories.

At the window, she listened to the screech and grind of the boxcars rolling through Asheville. The wind is what she wanted to hear. With all her might she listened for the wind he wrote about. She waited. Then: between the train sounds and Haywood street traffic outside her second-floor window—the wind, it came in a rustle of branches and leaves; and it swept back her brown bangs like a steel comb that never touched her skin, giving her tingly goose pimples from head to toe.

She dressed in the dark, excited, for she must go to him on this first night of October that's so close to his birthday on the third.

Ann Bruin transferred from the Portland Public Library. Single, good references, professional resume, intelligent—was about all her co-workers knew about the quiet girl from Portland.

She was so quiet: her three neighbors in her Haywood brownstone didn't know anything about her or hear her leave her apartment so late at night.

  She was wearing her hooded dark brown jogging suit with the hood covering her long brown straight hair. Her dark olive skin looked French; her brown eyes were intelligent and wary of strangers. Everyone was a stranger to Ann. Her 5'9" full-bodied frame moved gracefully on strong legs that had lived outdoors, hiked the Pacific Northwest and Europe with a boyfriend she dated for a year after high school.

  —He is a good writer, she thought, as she turned west for two blocks, headed for the Riverside Cemetery.

  —Better than I thought, and certainly better than some, she smiled and thought about the last time she saw him:

  The main library was always busy in the fall. Ann was a new employee at the reference desk when this man came up to her, looking as if he was lost and wanting help. He said:

  —Hi, my name is D. H. Dayne. I have three novels that are in your library system. I'd really like to know how they're doing. Would you please see if they're circulating?

She hoped he didn't notice her fingers trembling on the way to the keyboard. She had just started working at this job and wanted so much to act mature and look confident. She could look thirty and act forty. She would dress in black and browns most days; the dark colors were striking against her olive skin, with her long hair pinned in a bun above those brown eyes that had seen so much in her twenty-three years.

  She checked her system branches' circulation figures on the computer. On the first title she read the results to the anxious writer:

  —*Ledges* circulated two times in Arden, one time in Black Mountain, once in Weaverville, she said.

He left the reference desk before she could say anything. She knew he had to be in his 40's. He looked it, too, she thought.

The black iron gate to the cemetery was closed. Easily, she climbed it and vaulted herself over the top of the cold iron. She walked purposely along one of the many circuitous narrow drives that led to the back of the vast cemetery dwarfed by Carolina Pines. Now she can hear the wind roaring above her after flipping down her hood, passing row after row of granite and marble tombstones standing in a thousand different directions.

She read about his coming here to visit his brother's grave. It was yet some fifty steps till she reached the sacred earth of the man she knew so much about now, thanks to that writer in the library who checked out all his books and made her want to read him.

She even spent her second job getting paid to talk about Thomas Clayton Wolfe, who now lived here at her feet on the edge of the Wolfe family plot in Riverside Cemetery.

She knelt and raked the earth on his grave with her palm, lightly brushing the short grass six feet above the man who taught her to see and feel with all her being. Her brown eyes were closed. She laid out upon his grave, like an angel on her side, until she turned slowly onto her back, letting her eyes goes high into the blackness above her. She was remembering the day she watched him writing at a table in the far corner of the library by the microfiche viewers, away from the homeless men and loafers who came in just to sleep with magazines on their soiled clothing.

Not once did she let him catch her watching him for the two hours he wrote so feverishly with his head craned so low, his pencil moving so fast and furious. And she saw him curse when he broke the lead off his pencil, but, like a surgeon, prepared for such emergencies: he snatched another pencil from his black leather azel and continued writing without losing a beat. It was so beautiful, she thought at the time.

When she saw him leave the library she noticed he dropped a balled clump of paper into the trash can before exiting. She retrieved it and read it during her hot bath, which she always took right after work. In her bathtub, she opened the two pages of white typing paper, carefully—pages that were covered with his words on one side and then crumpled into a tight ball.

She read all the words in a whisper, as if she were reading something stolen. The words reminded her of Thomas Wolfe and his brother Ben, who was buried nearby. They were words about two brothers who were eight years apart; the older was a senior in high school; the younger brother was in grade school. They lived with their mother and sister in a new two-bedroom apartment complex near the Missouri River in Nebraska called the Riverside Apartments.

Their sister was in high school and wanted her own room, without sharing one with her brothers; so, the boys slept in a walk-in closet that was just big enough to support the metal-framed bed that folded up into an accordion on wheels. The bed literally covered every square inch of space in the empty closet.

Ann was moved by the way he described sleeping in the closet in winter, then springtime. In winter, he likened it to sleeping in a breadbox that was coated on the inside with paint thinner and dead air. It was the elder brother who usually slept alone in the dark, unvented space, because he had kicked out his little brother for snoring. The younger brother gladly went into his mother's room and slept comfortably with a less grouchy roommate.

He went on to say how the older brother kept the door shut when he slept, for he did not like his life in high school, describing the older brother as nothing but a blushing athlete with buck teeth and a grown man's dick. That's why the dark closet fit him so perfectly.

And there was a paragraph she read over ten times, soaking in his words with her lavender bath beads. It was how he described the front entrance to their apartment building, and how it stirred him one spring day after school. He described the flecks of mud on the front of his pants as frozen chocolate pudding blemishes he noticed right then, when he bent down to scrape the bottom of his muddy soles from the unpaved sidewalk that ran for twenty yards to their building. And as he bent to inspect his pants, he caught the fragrance in the wet spring wind of several scarlet begonias blooming in caked mud near the cement steps. In an instant, the sweet fragrance had mixed with the mud, the river, and the end of his boyhood, for he hurried to his closet before others arrived home and discovered what other boys his age had discovered much earlier than he.

Then, in the bottom left corner of the crumpled paper, after the closet scene, there was this library statistic he printed: Americans spend $300 billion a year on legalized gambling— enough money to fund public libraries for 75 years.

Ann knew that was a quote on a library book marker at the library checkout counter.

Now, still on her back, gazing dreamily up into the darkness, she thought how lonely he must be to spend his time writing alone, thinking of such things. He was much like the man whose bones are below her, under this timeless and dark earth he cherished to the last degree with every fiber of his being. But she had her own theory about Asheville's favorite son: She believed Tom suffered from a heavy burden of psychological time, which she thought was linked to a false sense of identity loaded with guilt and non-forgiveness.

Yes, she believed this famous writer who penned such novels as *Look Homeward, Angel, Of Time And The River, You*

an't Go Home Again, suffered from a serious and dangerous
ental illness. His characters were never at ease, always anxious;
ey seemed tense, stressed out—all forms of fear caused by too
uch worry. On the other hand, his writing conveys something of
 enigma that dispels such a claim, because she knows that
gativity is caused by an accumulation of psychological time, the
me rigid belief system operating under the implicit assumption
at the highest good lies in the future, and, therefore, the end
stifies the means.

Ann Bruin believed that war is a chilling example of that,
at is, how belief in a future heaven creates a present hell. But she
ew of no writer or artist who lived in the present moment nearly
 much as Wolfe. How could such a man be loaded down with
ch guilt and resentment, and yet, live in the present moment? she
ondered aloud.

Yes, this young woman from Portland had learned so well
at if you learn from the past and move on, you are using clock
ne. However, if you dwell on your past mistakes, mentally, and
el guilt, it has become psychological time and manifests one day
to disease or illness if not handled.

It was October's first morning, and today is the day he had
orked for. Dwayne slept well after his walk to Tom's cabin. For
o long he has been avoiding this move. It's not so much the
nount of time, three years, but rather, it's what he's been doing
ring these thousand days that makes it so damn important to him.
or five days a week for 50 weeks a year, he's been selling his
oks to libraries via telemarketing. Nearly five thousand US/CN
raries carry all three of his books. About eight libraries a day,
ipped by himself by the USPS, with only a 5% return rate. Not
d, considering his books look self-published, right off his
pewriter. He tried to cover that in the creative phone pitch that's
ved him from a disastrous 25% return rate, at the very least. He

called his pitch his "save."

As he now walked up the hill, past cabins like his, except many have smoke pouring out of their chimneys, he recites his save, to himself, on his way to his mailbox, even though he knows the mail has not come yet.

—Oh, my librarians tell me to tell you that when you put my books on your new-book table...your patrons will know they're self-published...because the font is right off my typewriter. Many tell me to tell you to just give them a chance, for the stories are gems; and once I get a reader, they start to circulate. That's what my librarians tell me to tell you. Thank you for this opportunity. And find me a bunch of readers, please. Bye, bye.

He unlocked his mailbox. Nothing. This is the last day he is giving this lifestyle he's created. If nothing comes in the mail, as usual, he will make that drastic change today. As he headed back down the hill, he thought about how he's been a screenwriter for these twenty years since his first novel bombed. Eight original screenplays he wrote. He had pitched some to Hollywood producers—nothing. He had submitted queries, sample pages and entire scripts a thousand times to agents and producers—nothing. They were all lying to him for he would turn page 20 upside down or omit, and nothing would be mentioned of it; he would put a paper clip on page 20. Same thing. They had never read that far. Liars.

He's never had one good reader (except in Maine). Forty-two months ago D. H. Dayne turned his script *The Spanking* into a novel. He had to know if his movies have an audience. They do. Two hundred thousand readers after two years. A half-million in three years.

Yes, he had gone through the back door, around the mainstream publishing loop and their stable of writers they feed the public. Yes, after three years of selling his books to his outlets, he will make this change.

When he opened his cabin door, he saw the main reason he's going to make this big change: REJECTION. He scanned his front room walls, where on nearly every square inch of wall space, is a note or rejection letter from agents, producers, publishers, writing contests, and even notes from librarians who returned his books to him with their negative comments. After putting on his glasses, he went over to the main wall and picked out a note from a librarian, which he read aloud:

—Mr. Dayne: I bought your books with the intention of keeping them. Then I attempted to read your first book and could not get through it, for you wore out the word smirk, using it way too often. I am returning your books and do not wish to purchase any more of your future work.

Dwayne smirked at the note and moved his eyes to a rejection slip the size of a fortune cookie that simply said: sorry.

He knows that the contest results from his script *Ledges* should be in today's mail, and that what he will get is more of this wall of rejection. Then: he stepped back from the wall and began to chant one of the many mantras he used to quiet his mind:

—AH...OHH...MM...

Louder he chanted and sang:

—AHH...OHH...MM...I accept life!

Next, Dwayne stood with his legs apart, and after he removed his glasses he began to swing his upper body back and forth, letting his eyes go while keeping them open, he chanted:

—Let things go!   Go with the flow!

Then louder:

—Oh, Great Spirit! Land, Sky, Sun, and Sea! You are inside and all around me!

Still swinging, slowly, back and forth, he chanted with a deeper pitch, moving up in higher notes when he imagined each of the seven chakras and the color for each. At his tailbone he imagined red and chanted EH (as in red) for three exhalations.

Above that, near his navel, he saw the color orange and chanted OHH (as in hope). Then, up to his diaphragm he saw gold and chanted AUM. Next: to the heart chakra, he bathed it in green and pink and vibrated his upper chest with AHH for the same three exhalations. Then, the throat chakra. He saw azure blue while singing UUH (as in blue). On his third breath: his phone rang; he let his answering machine take the call, not distracted at all during his image of blue, then purple and violet for the last two chakras a some librarian from Ohio wanted to order a copy of his three bool and rambled on about how she was interested in having him for a book signing.

Still swinging, he worked back down in scale from the top of his head to his tailbone. Then, he kept swinging but remained quiet for five minutes, letting his eyes go with the flow of the roon with every swing. Just then: the roar of the mailman's engine race up the hill, a sound so familiar and distinct to those waiting for the delivery of important things.

He continued to swing, knowing these affirmations and rituals for the spirit were manifested in his daily living—only because he is an American writer, the loneliest and bravest of vocations, for no one but a writer values his musings scribbled in a thousand places, at all hours of the day and night, 365 days a year. He writes mostly at night in order to get at the heart of what he is trying to say. He uses the daylight hours for taking in what he wants to say; this is the charged energy that brings things to him while he channels his aggression to market his books to librarians, like the hunter.

He learned from Tom to stay away from that American tra at night to socialize in dark bars, where his people hide their bigge of fears–aloneness.

He climbed the hill again when he knew the man had been to his box. Each step took him closer to his biggest move—if it's another rejection, or if the box is empty. He opened his box and

...ed out the letter he'd been expecting from the Universal ...eenwriting Contest, its gold-colored letters on the envelope ...rkling in his hand over junk mail.

He tore into the letter and read it while walking downhill; ...opening line was as familiar as the path underfoot:

Dear Mr. Dayne: Thank you for your submission. You ...rk was well received however, not as a finalist. We wish you ...od luck in placing your writing in the future. Keep writing.

—Keep writing, he mumbled cynically.

Once inside his cabin, he quietly took down every single ...ction notice on his walls, crumpling each one into a ball and ...ing it drop to the floor as if he were prepared for this moment.

Born To Love Him

At noon, Ann Bruin parked her late-model Escort in the Thomas Wolfe parking area next to the Wolfe boardinghouse Dixieland, made famous in Tom's first novel *Look Homeward, Angel*. She always wore black at her second job; it seemed to fit the mood of the dark interior and her somber narration as a tour guide in the vast 2-story home furnished in early American antique once used by the Wolfe household and its boarders. For three bucks one could tour the Wolfe house today.

She wore black today, with high-laced Pilgrim shoes that mother Julia Wolfe and her female boarders would have worn in th early 1900s. Ann wore only a trace of rouge on her cheekbones, n other makeup; this trace of rouge changed her countenance totally For Ann is a chameleon who can change with the seasons and colors adorned, depending on her mood. She can wear this black ankle-length linen dress with a black sweater riding her shoulders above a cream-colored blouse, all spotless and clean on her combined meager salaries of $240.00 a week, six bucks an hour fo forty hours a week.

Her intent is to look thirty years old at the library and here. When she ascended the front steps to the Dixieland L-shaped porch, she glanced to her left and saw no tourists waiting on the high-back rocking chairs. She dialed the security code near the front door to disarm the alarm before she unlocked the front door with two different keys on the turquoise key chain she bought at th Little America gift shop in Wyoming on her drive to Asheville thre months ago.

She had read all of Tom's books when she was in Oregon; what she didn't know about his life she had learned from listening to Scott Wauklen, her boss and the director of the Wolfe Memoria undation. She had given some four dozen tours in two months, ith Scott usually there to alternate with her. But today she will ork alone because Scott is in Raleigh lobbying for money for a ixieland paint job, inside and out.

Today will be busy and each day busier, especially on the ird, Tom's birthday, his centennial birthday even though he's been ead for over sixty years. She hoped Scott would return tomorrow planned. A tour is on every hour, and Ann will give them all day. It will be the first time she's solo; usually she or Scott ould be downstairs to answer questions and to take in money for olfe souvenirs, mostly black and white postcards of Tom that are old in the little gift shop across from the parlor just off to the right f the front door.

It took her ten minutes to turn on all the lights in the twenty ooms of the boardinghouse. When she was upstairs in the room ext to Ben's room, she pulled open the curtain and saw him anding outside in front of the house. She moved back, out of ew from the window and watched him. She whispered his name herself:

—Dwayne Dayne.

he watched him remove one of his shoes and put his socked foot side one of Tom's huge size 15 bronze shoes welded to the front dewalk. Soon, both of his feet were inside the bronze shoes; he's oking down at them, until: his eyes startled her as they shot up to en's room, the room next to her's on the second floor. He was oking for something important. His eyes stayed there, fixed on en's room.

When she left the window she noticed she'd been holding er breath; her heart was racing. She wanted to run down to him d tell him she read all his books, and that she liked them. But, ; she decided not to, he might get the wrong idea.

—Besides, he's too old for me, she reminded herself as she tered Ben's room and raked open the curtains, this time hoping he saw her in the window. She looked down to see if she could see him on the porch, but then she heard the tinkling silver bell above the front door downstairs.

—Oh, my God, he's here, she nearly blurted out loud.

Quickly, she straightened her hair in the porcelain-framed mirror in the bathroom off Ben's room before heading downstairs.

She could see him standing with his hands in his coat pockets behind the velvet rope just outside the Wolfe parlor. He appeared a bit glum to her, as if he was thinking about something that bothered him. He is surprised to see the reference librarian here as the tour guide.

—Hi!, he smiled. You work here, too?

—Yes, she smiled back, looking so alive and attractive to him in his eyes, she stopped breathing.

This moment was numb to him because of the wholesale rejections librarians gave him by the thousands, combined with the recent rejection at his mailbox, and, here was this beautiful young woman he was not able to feel if she was attracted to him.

—If she's thirty or younger..she's not interested in me, he told himself before telling her:

—I know I'm too early for a tour. I was hoping I could walk around a bit on my own; of course, after I've paid my three bucks, he smiled.

She thought his smile was dead, half there, and if Scott were here she'd have to say no, but:

—Yeah, sure, it's okay.

He handed her three dollars he had ready in his fist as if he'd planned it. She noticed everything. Even the dampness of the bills he handed her told her he was anxious about something.

—My name's Dwayne.

He extended his right hand to shake hers, saying, as he craned his head down to her as if to get her name from her. She wanted to tell him that she knew his name. That she read his books. And he would say:

—Really?

She would smile and add:

—And when you were in the library checking on how they were circulating..I had them at home..and I was reading them with all my heart. They were wonderful. I loved them.

Instead, she acted shy and told him her name is Ann.

—Hi, Ann..you a Wolfe fan?

—Yes, I am, she smiled.

An awkward pause, until he said:

—May I go upstairs now and look around?

—Sure.

She watched him walk away, to and up the narrow and dark stairway. He appeared lost to her, as if he was not sure why he was here. She went over to the display case counter in the gift shop. From her waist pocket she removed a tiny vile of essential oil, Joy, a sweet fragrance of lemons and rosebush. She smelled the fragrance balanced to produce the chemical reaction in the brain for joy. She dashed a couple drops onto her palm and traced it from her chin to the nape of her slender neck before breathing in deeply the joy left in her palm. As she looked down to her reflection in the counter glass:

He knew exactly where he was going. He called it Tom's room, though Tom didn't really have his own room in Dixieland; he was constantly changing sleeping rooms to accommodate his mother's boarders. This was the room next to Tom's brother Ben's room, the room where Ann viewed Dwayne standing in Tom's bronze shoes.

Dwayne stood at the same window, looking to the right at the balcony where Tom had snuck out to have his first fling, with an older woman, one of his mother's boarders who stayed in the adjoining room.

Dwayne unlatched the window lock and made sure the

window could be raised without trouble. There was no screen on the other side of the glass, and he saw no alarm wires. After he closed the window, he closed the latch just a bit, and could still open the window.

He turned and saw the narrow divan that Tom slept on, its length against the wall just inside the window. That dark walnut writing table was in the center of the room; it's doubtful he ever did any writing there. When Dwayne headed for Ben's room, he paused in the doorway as:

Ann stood at the bottom of the stairs, terrified of taking that first step. She wanted to say something clever or humorous to him because his writing was full of real/funny dialog from characters alive in interesting situations. And Ben was the name of his protagonist in *Ledges*. Now she had something to say to him, but she would wait for the right moment.

For thirty-five minutes she waited, until three middle-aged couples came in together for the first tour. They were from Boston and talked like the Yankees who stayed in Julia Wolfe's boarding-house.

Ann forgot about Dwayne upon entering Julia's expansive kitchen at the back of the house. After she showed them mother Wolfe's tiny servant's room, off the kitchen, where Julia slept, and the cubbyhole booth where the family dined, she led them upstairs.

She thought that surely he would hear them tramping up these creaking steps, making all this racket, yet she was puzzled as to why she was unable to hear him upstairs, for every step made on these old oak floors creaked and told of visitors.

She narrated purposely loud to warn him that they were coming. Control with her voice was hard for her to sustain. When she led them into Ben's room, she blushed fast, as surprised as the guests, to see a man asleep on Ben's bed; his head on a pillow at the head of the bed in the center, with his arms spread-eagle. They could hear a faint snore coming from his parted lips.

Ann leaned over at the side of the brass bed; she stood next to his shoes:

—Mr. Dayne. Wake up, Mr. Dayne.

He opened his eyes, relaxed at first, then bolted up, remembering where he was and explaining as he put on his shoes real fast:

—I'm sorry. I dozed off. I just wanted to know..I'm sorry, he repeated, while in the awkward silence he quickly smoothed out the bedding and straightened the pillow before exiting the room past the stupefied tourists and their guide.

As her tourists whispered and giggled in Ben's room about the man found asleep on Ben's bed, Ann ducked into the adjoining room to watch him walk away from Dixieland in a rush. Just then: she noticed the unlocked window right in front of her nose. She started to reach for the latch to lock it, but she stopped herself, deciding to leave it unlocked.

Later: he sat up and bounced a bit before lying back spread-eagle on the queen-sized mattress in the Winnebago RV Adventurer bedroom. This time he would not fall asleep, he told himself, still smiling at the faces he saw in Ben's room, gape-jawed like apes.

He closed his eyes and opened them, imagining what it's like to wake up in a motor home. He wondered if he could live in such a confining space, alone. It's either hit the road—or no life, stuck in some rented place that keeps my gypsy blood cold, and always yearning for greener grasses.

—Yes, I can see this, he smiled, knowing this is the biggest move he's ever made.

Dwayne's made up his mind to commit to two years doing book signings where his books are circulating. Still on his back, he had this problem of being truly alone. His thoughts came out:

When my brother died, I was devastated, angry, horror-stricken to my core. No thoughts like, "He's with God now";

"He's in a better place"; "God must've wanted him with Him." It was more like, "He's better off dead."

Before he died, I thought I was under some kind of boyhood umbrella that was lined with some God-like protection He put there to keep me from harm. Yes, I believed this god-like figure was some benevolent Father, always up there in the sky, watching over little me. When bad weather came my way, I was saved, every single time...by Him. I'm talking twenty thousand saves from all kinds of pernicious situations and people, and even bad weather.

I was lucky. With all those chips stacked in God's favor, the moment I heard my brother was gone, I walked away from His table, not wanting to play His game anymore. How could someone so powerful, someone who saved me so many times, let my brother's life end in such a cruel way? Or better yet, I want to know how He could allow such a thing to happen if He's supposed to be so loving and omnipotent.

So, now, it's glorious October in Asheville, in the Blue Ridge...and I'm truly alone without that umbrella. That's how my brother's death changed me. I must change the way I live. I must. I cannot live this same way. I'm gonna get rained on now and then, from now on, I know, but at least I know there's no umbrella or any security from the cradle to the grave.

That's one of the reasons why I may never be a writer/in, and why my writing will be dismissed as nothing, since I could never stay in third person tense after he died. To me, third person is like God narrating the story. I don't believe in Him anymore. So, I will tell my stories in first and third person, confusing whoever. And who cares? Confusion is a high state of being. Today is confusing. I'm sure many are confused about how God can let box-cutters kill some six thousand people.

Maybe because it's His world. He does what He wants; allows what He wants to happen. Well, you won't catch me talking o Him anymore...in first or third person. I'll write how I want in His world; and sell what I write until I'm gone. If He doesn't approve—I can be taken out. But I will not complain along the way. This is my path now...in my world.

Public libraries in 49 states and Canada shelf his books; he could pick and choose where he wants to go. He always wanted to travel with the seasons—and now is his chance, especially to explore Canada. He told his parents in Phoenix he wanted to do this while he still has the energy to do it. An RV would get him out more and certainly force him to meet more people.

Asheville was like any other place he'd lived. Before long, he'd been seen writing in his favorite spots—restaurants and coffeehouses—by a public who learned from repetition to stay away from the writer, a strange vocation the working public will never understand in America.

Roaming from town to town, from library to library, in his bookmobile, he can sell his books at book signings and spend more time on his next book, cranking out two a year, perhaps. Sometimes he may decide to market his books via the phone from a rental cabin for a month or so. Then, move to another place he wants to experience, and market his books for another month until his five thousand libraries shelf his new book. The best part: he can now get much more writing time. Who knows what will come?

—I'm a gypsy, he smiled. I'll survive, he told himself, unafraid but anxious about this move.

He got off the bed in the back of the Winnebago and checked the size of the bathroom again with its tub/shower. He liked hot baths.

The kitchen/dining/living room was in the middle of the RV; he liked the table booth and the leather furniture with no carpeting, for his allergy to dust was always hard on him in the summer. There was plenty of space to store his books under the frame of the

Adventurer. And the cab was deep and separate from the living area of the unit.

—Can I live in this? he asked.

Again, he asked himself if he could live here as he sat at the booth with his palms flat on the table, his eyes taking in the space he would have to commit to for two years.

Just then: his reverie went back to his unclaimed first novel, not the plot.

In 1978, he was 25 when he found a printer in Phoenix to print his first novel. His writing wasn't ready or good enough to be published. But he was ready to be read. Something drove him to borrow two grand from his uncle, to give to the printer he finally found who was willing to work with him. There was something good that the printer saw in Dwayne that allowed him to give the writer a break and front Dwayne the books on consignment; he could pay for the books as he sold them.

No other writer was as prepared as he to market his own book for five bucks a copy. His cost was $1.25 a book; but there was still that problem: his writing wasn't good enough to be sold at retail outlets; he would have to sell his book one at a time to his readers. And, he knew just how and just where to go—businesses. Every business in his path he would enter and pitch quick, whoever he could talk to. Strip malls were good, as long as the owner or the manager wasn't too busy with customers. Beauty shops, locksmiths, copy businesses, delis, pet shops, and a thousand other types of small businesses are perfect for a small-ticket item. Phoenix was loaded with strip malls.

He was young and handsome and had the energy to withstand eight hours of rejection, pounding pavement with his handleless sales case stuffed with books, riding his left hip, keeping his right hand free to open that door that would lead to his one good reader:

—Hi! I'm a writer selling my own novel, door-to-door, for
ve bucks a copy. Do you or anyone close to you read novels...I
ope?

was those two simple words at the end that broke the tension.
he way he said, "I hope," with a half-grin that usually got a
huckle out of his prospect. Then, he'd hand his prospect a copy of
is paperback, saying:

—There's a summary/review on the back cover.

le watched their eyes read the summary about his protagonist
eonard, the baby boy who was abandoned on a boxcar and
escued by the Federal systems Inspector Barney, who would return
wenty years later and rescue, again, this twitching and stammering
oung man who was illegally adopted by an abusive couple in a
ansas hick town called Hixson.

Dwayne had spent a lot of time and thought on writing a
ood summary. When the prospect finished reading the summary,
ist as he or she would riff the pages and begin reading some
assage in the middle of the book:

—It's right off my typewriter. It's five dollars and I'd love
o sign one to you or to someone as a gift.

en to fifteen times a day: they would say yes and buy his book.
bout two books an hour for eight hours a day; however, with
riving and walking time, he probably had about five hours of
ctual selling time, yielding three books an hour, average. Just
urvival. The best part about it: he was able to make his rent and
rans Am payment, keeping his car Rusty parked under a canvas
ar cover, while getting some readers along the way.

Then: he tried selling to some single-family homes in
hoenix housing divisions that were close together, many in cul de
acs. Residents yielded about the same numbers, except he would
et more fatigued from dehydration and the relentless Phoenix sun;
arking dogs and rejection were hard on him. What drained him
he most: when his prospects peered at him from behind their peek-

-43-

holes—he had to look relaxed, friendly, cool as a Mexican cucumber. Usually the door opened:

—Hi! My name's Dwayne Dayne. I'm selling my novel, door-to-door, for five dollars a copy. Do you read novels?

He would split the day between businesses and residences, usually with a half-hour break at a fast-food restaurant. But the days grew hotter and longer. He knew something had to change, he felt it in his bowels. He blamed it on the sun and that special sauce on the Big Mac when he was trapped in a residential cul de sac after lunch with no public bathroom in sight. He filled his black polyester dress slacks after failing to hold it any longer on his brisk walk back to his black Trans Am, that would soon have the electric sun roof open on the way to a gas station.

He quit having lunch and started losing weight. Something had to change besides his diet. It did. Still fearful of shitting his pants in the territory, a prospect, while reading his back cover summary, told Dwayne about a newborn baby who was abandoned on an Amtrak car in San Diego early this morning, and how it reminded her of his character Leonard.

Dwayne bought a paper right away and read the article about the abandoned girl nurses named Hope. Later that day: Dwayne put together a laminated 8 x 10 sales presentation folder that displayed the baby Hope's newspaper article, and he hit the bricks, calling on businesses first.

Yes, Dwayne's leading character Leonard began his life as baby Hope, but Hope, the abandoned baby girl was not his main connection to his novel. In the story: his protagonist Leonard was involved with a Helpline in San Francisco that raised money for good causes when a little girl, Amy, in the city, is killed by an abusive parent. Leonard writes a TV commercial about the girl's tragic death, using Stevie Wonder's song *Isn't She Lovely* to drive home a poignant message that kept the Helpline phones ringing with donations. It was the young girl Amy who was killed by an

busive parent, who gave Dwayne his connection to child abuse in
is book—not baby Hope.

Every *White Shoulders* prospect heard about the baby girl
Iope, and when this self-published writer pledged to raise one
Iousand dollars for a trust fund in Hope's name from the sales of
is novel, sales averaged twenty books per day vs. ten or fifteen at
Ie most. Hope made all the difference: his energy went up from
Icreased sales, and his altruism was helping a good cause.

The public was so receptive, he found more receptionists
Igging into their purses for loose change, spending their lunch
Ioney to buy a book in order to help little Hope.

Dwayne learned to work security-heavy office buildings in
owntown Phoenix by starting at the top floor and working his way
own by using the stairs. His goal was to hit bottom without a
ecurity guard escorting him out. Before Hope: he rarely made it
ast three or four floors. After Hope: he often would have to make
trip to his car to refill his sales case with more books. For now,
arely did his prospects rat on him and call security. He told them
e was going to give Hope a thousand-dollar trust fund from his
ook sales. This made Dwayne feel like his character—a hero.

—A hero, Dwayne mumbled. Everyone wants to be a hero.

Dwayne came out of his reverie staring from ceiling to
oor, then he sat up straight and looked hard to the back of the RV
o the front of the cab.

—Can I live here? He asked out loud.
ust then: the RV main door opened. The RV salesman's face
miled at his prospect when he asked Dwayne if he wanted to go
or a spin.

On the test drive, Dwayne asked all the important questions:
Iow do I replenish the water supply? How do I dump the waste?
)oes it start to smell like an outhouse in here?

Behind the wheel, Dwayne thought it felt right, not as

cumbersome on turns as he thought it would be; it just didn't feel like a big lug. A grand a month would be his payment with nothing down, as long as his credit was good.

He told the salesman he wanted to sleep on it, and he'd let him know tomorrow.

Dwayne knew he wanted to be on the road by the Third, on Tom's birthday; and besides, his rent at the cabin was due on the third, plus his new book would be ready from his printer in Winston-Salem. The question was: Was he ready for this two-year commitment? His first book took two years to sell. Would this be another dead end?

How smart and final that would be, to drive down the mountain just as Tom rode the train out of Asheville, headed east to library book signings, on the way to a sparkling new life, meeting new people, seeing the places they live in, eating their food that sustains them, and, the best part, moving on to new territory to write about.

Yes, Dwayne has missed his life as a gypsy, selling on the road. This time he won't struggle for money. He has money. He can stay in a motel if he wants and stretch out in a hot bath, or rent a cabin for a month whenever he wants.

And now he can get out of this lonely heartsickness that creeps into his bones at night, soaks into his bloodstream and saturates his brain with this sadness about being...comfortable. In one of his books he had written about how a man needs change as much as a woman needs security. But, most men tend to saddle themselves with the feminine need to be taken care of—and there goes his aliveness, that sense of danger and pioneerism his great grandparents must have known.

Yes, again, he can be a pioneer, a road warrior peddling his books, a stranger in every town. It was also clear: he must find a gypsy woman to be complete. He's tried the other: living in one place for "her"; it didn't work for "him." It's high time to be true o the male warrior he's neglected for way too long. He knows hat 99% of the women will not be interested in him; "she" will be n the 1% of independent women who can move with him without he security of roots and family.

And she must be strong, not dependent on him or family or riends or anything else that will make her long for something other han the life she can manifest for the two of them. She will love hildren and animals, in that order, yet she will have none to care or. She will love nature and solitude as a healer; her mere resence will bring out the light in others, casting away impatience, ruelty, and every ounce of pride. Most of all: in her eyes, he will e a writer/in, and she will expect him to act like one—confident nd alive.

—I will find her, he mumbled, as he sat in Lawn Boy at the RV dealership.

Before driving away in his blue sardine can, he surveyed vhat a sharp drop in temperature had done to the distant trees overing the Blue Ridge. Red, gold, orange, and yellow flames that orce the eyes to forget the azure blue Carolina sky and behold this irestorm of colors in all directions. These have to be the colors of omance, the colors of love before pain, the colors of sweet nemories before loss. For these colors will diminish and fall, eaving but the woods of winter gray. Autumn has this power of olor that keeps him aware that love is possible, and that one day is writing can be validated by that vicious loop of publishers that ontinues to grind out the same stories from the same stable of vriters, letting in a new voice only when their glorious/perfunctor-ous vision allows us all to see it in print.

Yes, D. H. Dayne might be better off not even thinking bout the publishing world that locks him out; it will only hurt his ext book and cause him to grind his back teeth together, which ives his face such a serious demeanor that even people he was riendly with would stay away.

Inside Lawn Boy: Dwayne tilted his rear-view mirror so he could only see his eyes when he said:

—Dwayne Harvey Dayne...do you want to live in an RV? He waited, paying attention to his breath, letting his exhalations out for eight beats while his eyes stayed on the hills in the mirror. He whispered:

—Tell me.

That evening: it gets dark early now in October. Lawn Boy was parked outside Riverside Cemetery near the main entrance. Deep into the expansive cemetery so close to that narrow land right beside Tom's grave, Dwayne sat with his legs crossed under him. From two filled bulging plastic grocery bags, he removed his balled rejection letters, slips and notes. Every single one of those balls of rejection he stacked and shaped into one pyramid in front of Tom's modest headstone. The stack was about two feet high when the last piece of balled paper was gently placed at the top. At this point, he was glad he had tossed about half of them away when he received them in the dozens of cities, towns, and places he's called home.

He peeked around Tom's marker, making sure he was alone before he struck a match and lit the bottom of the pile in several places. The flames grew fast, illuminating the inscription of Thomas Wolfe's stone and the neighboring markers of his family, all clustered together as if they were buried standing up.

As the fire crackled and glowed orange, he had to scoot back on the frosty grass a safe distance from the rising heat. He thought about how his favorite writer must have been here several times to visit the ghost of brother Ben and his father who made his living with his massive paws, chiseling these very letters and numbers on tombstones of the Asheville dead.

Next: Dwayne removed a writing pen from his shirt pocket, and while he held it up in front of the flames, he said, with intensity:

—Tom...I swear with all my being...on your grave...to keep writing and selling my books...until they are recognized. And I promise to live my life to the fullest, every day...from this moment on. May your spirit be with me so I can see all the ghosts of past, present and future...so I'm able to write the stories I'm destined to write.

Just then: Dwayne violently stabbed the point of his pen into the earth above Tom's grave, leaving the pen standing there with about half the pen in the black soil.

On his feet, he stood before his flames of rejection with his head bowed, his chin pointed down to the pen that was six feet above Tom's bones. Then, tears began to fall with his silent earnest prayer whispered with quivering chin:

—Father, Mother, Great Spirit, God...creator of all things, Brother Tom...show me how to sustain on my quest to be a writer/in. I cannot do it without you...and will not resist your plan. Help me to see it, please...so I may become this writer/in and somehow help others along the way.

It was the penultimate moment to open his eyes. In dead fire: he saw what he should do next; he smiled at the heap of black ashes beginning to scatter and crumble away in tufts of breezes blowing warm from the south.

Later that night: he looked at his watch while seated behind Lawn Boy's moonlit windshield and turned off his CD player after listening to Chris Rea's song *Windy Town* while parked in the Dixieland parking lot. It is just after midnight and but 24 hours until Tom's birthday. He knows he could never do this on the third, as now he can still hear Rea's train shunting down by the river. He could really feel that all things seemed to be going better now after his commitment made over Tom's dead body. That was on his mind when he said:

—Tell me when to go in.

He began breathing deep from his lower belly, real deep.

He could see his seven chakras in ascending then descending colors, images of each chakra blazing so clearly, like some kind of crystal neon. He knew that the pattern of imagery must be exact and in the correct order for healing to manifest. When finished: he gazed up to the top of Lawn Boy's windshield and could see the jutting dormer windows of brother Ben's room on the front end of the big house on the second floor.

This is the third time in D. H. Dayne's life that he's lived in Asheville, and he knew it would be the last.

Ben's room was the key to his freedom. If he can let go tonight, his life in an RV will be a fun experience—instead of another way to hide this terrible thing that keeps him numb and unable to soar in the present.

From Lawn Boy's trunk he got a pair of brown cotton gloves; he walked toward the front of the dark boardinghouse and over to the side of the house farthest from Ben's room.

Across from Dixieland in the ten-story Hilton, at the side lobby entrance door facing Dixieland, she watched him climb to the second floor by using the trellis. She'd been waiting for over two hours, watching for him. She saw him crouch atop the porch roof, making his way to the veranda in the dark, until he reached the window she left unlocked for him. He went in through that window and vanished into the blackness inside the Wolfe house.

She waited, thinking about his novel *The Paper Man*. She thought of the unrequited love he wrote about, between Harvey and Josie, comparing it to her own yearning to be held by an older man, perhaps the way her father might have held her if her life had been different. She felt there was no need to be afraid of him, for if a man can write so tenderly about love—there is nothing to fear...but intimacy.

She had the key to the door clenched tightly in her fist, but

orgot it was there until she pushed open the lobby door with her
vaist and fell into the crisp October air in her Nikes and black
ogging suit.

She let herself into Dixieland, quietly, without tinkling the
ell above the door. She had left the alarm off, purposely for him.
he could feel her heart beating as she lit a candle and carried it to
he bottom of the stairs. When Ann looked up, all the way to the
op of the winding staircase, she thought of the song by Chris Rea,
I Can Hear Your Heartbeat in his novel *The Paper Man*. She knew
he song so well: it played in her head as she climbed slowly, feeling
ke an intruder for being here now; and, she felt silly for buying all
he music he had put into his stories.

She kept telling herself that he wouldn't hurt her. At the
op of the stairs, she knew where to go: Ben's room, where she
ound him during her tour. But, then, before her candle's light
eached the doorway to Ben's room, she could hear his deep
reathing coming from that room. She questioned why she was
eally there and what she would say to him. Then:

She made her move into the room and saw his shoes on the
loor again. When she raised the candle, hot wax dripped onto her
rembling fingers, causing her to drop the candle, which she
xtinguished when it hit the floor.

He didn't bolt up; when he opened his eyes to her, she was
urprised by what she said, and in this low voice she had never used
efore:

—Did you know I left the window unlocked for you?

—No, he smiled. Will you help me?

Vithout thinking, she nodded yes.

—Lie beside me, he whispered.

he removed her shoes with her heels, then she laid next to him on
he same pillow. Her body trembled next to his like some rat
errier; then, when he extended his left hand for her to hold: she did.

—I knew your name was Ann from your name tag at the

-51-

library. Where are you from?

—Portland...Oregon.

—Why'd you come here?

—You mean here, tonight, or Asheville?

—Both.

—I moved to Asheville to get away from my parents. To be independent. I had to get out on my own.

—Uh huh. Why'd you come here tonight?

She whispered her answer to him:

—I don't know. Maybe because I read your books. I really don't know.

—Why do you come into Ben's room?

—You know Ben died in this room...on this bed, he said.

—Of tuberculosis.

—Yes. I believe when Tom saw his brother dying it was the beginning of his own death. My only brother John killed himself last December.

—I'm so sorry.

—I believe Ben was Tom's main reason for returning to Asheville. To resolve the cruelty of seeing his proud brother die. was the same with me...a proud brother...an untenable rescue...the same stuff that choked Tom's heart to a shriveled clod of torn tissue when he lived hard and burnt out. I came to Asheville to get away from my dying brother. I ran away to get away from him and his God-forsaken pain that I must've known would kill him one day. So I ran.

Ann spoke to the ceiling, with him, in a whisper:

—That old saying: "You can't choose your relatives?" I believe we do. We choose them in order to learn the lessons we failed to learn in past lives. And if that's not true: then God, this universal creator of all...is responsible for all the bad things in this world, too. He can't just take credit for the good things and get away with it.

—I'm angry at God for letting my brother take his life. I ave to let go of that anger...or it will destroy me. I also have to let o of a belief system that deep down I did not believe in. That's hat the death of a loved one does, it tests your faith. I had none, ally. From the moment I found out he was gone—I realized I had faith at all. I know I'm here to let go of my brother so I can e. I must forgive him for what he did to himself and my mother. ow, the only thing that can help my mother heal...is for me to rgive him and put all my creative energy into becoming a ublished writer, recognized by the publishing loop, a writer/in I ll it.

—I've looked up your books in our library system. They e in many libraries...and circulate well. They are good stories... lf-published or not. You are a writer.

—Yes, I am a writer, but not a good writer, he laughed. aybe I'm supposed to be self-published forever...like the most nbitious writer ever. It always comes back to how I didn't put ly energy into my brother. It all went into my fiction.

—If you hadn't, you wouldn't be a wrier.

—I know. But now I know there's a door that leads to a e in which I can write often and help people along the way. I ant to reach my brother's spirit...here...tonight...and he will lead e through this door that makes me this writer/in.

They remained quiet for a while, still holding hands while reathing deeply. They listened to the wind blowing leaves of gold utside Ben's windows, the house creaking from its force and made oluble by the late hour.

—You must've been sent to me, he whispered, as he stared Ben's high ceiling covered in darkness. Dwayne breathed deeply id continued in a whisper:

—My brother John was like Ben, though my brother was ght years younger than me.

—How was he like Ben? she whispered.

—His eyes were bright blue...on fire. They would burn you when he leaned close to you to make his point. His lungs were weak, like Ben's. Asheville taught me that lungs are life, the taking-in of life, wanting to live...to breathe.

He didn't notice that Ann's hand had perspired onto his palm and between his fingers as he continued:

—The biggest personality trait they shared was pride. I'm sure you know that Tom wrote about his proud brother. I personally feel that Tom's best writing was about Ben. But he never wrote about how pride kills...how pride is the miasmic cesspool of life-choking resentment that clouds and smears your identity...until something dies.

Ann remained still, listening to his words:

—I could've rescued my brother instead of lecturing him about getting on his medication for bi-polar. No, I'm not blaming myself for his death, though I feel guilt for being self absorbed in my writing and marketing my books. I know that if I put half that same energy into him and his problem, he'd be here with me and ready to hit the road with me.

—Where are you going? she asked.

—I don't know. That's why I'm here.

—I know someone who can help you, she whispered after she turned her head to him.

—Who?

—Her name's Marjorie. She does this neuro-emotional release that really gets to the source of your feelings and allows you to let go of them. I had one treatment when I first moved here. It really did help me to let go of some old stuff and find out more about myself. That's true healing.

—How'd you find her?

—I saw her flyer at the library.

—Could I see her tomorrow? Or today?

—I don't know. I can call you and give you her number.

—Can I go with you to get the number when you leave?

—Sure.

he waited, hoping he wanted to leave now, because she knew that
 she were to be discovered here now, the librarian who referred
er to this job would find out, so she'd lose both of her jobs.

—Do you work tomorrow? he asked.

—No, I'm off for two days. Why?

—I just realized something. You are the one I was
upposed to meet here...to tell me about Marjorie. And it wasn't
om who sent you. It was my brother John. Yes! he exclaimed
nd sat up facing the window with his back to her.

—Your brother? she repeated.

—Yes, he whispered anxiously while discerning the full
arolina moon in Ben's window; he continued:

—that's what I believe. I have nothing to resolve with
om. A week after he died, I was driving in the desert in Southern
Iew Mexico. I'd been crying, thinking of him for a thousand miles.
couldn't hear anything on the radio but Spanish Christmas music
r country/western music he loved. When it was really quiet, I
ould hear my brother's voice in that excited tone of his–like when
e was a boy. He said: "No, Dwayne, don't worry about me. I'm
 a wonderful place with Pete and Kenny."

—Pete was like his adopted grandpa who he loved to
restle with; Pete taught my brother how to wrestle. Kenny was
y father, who died four years ago.

—You were half-brothers?

Ie turned to Ann, his eyes red and wet:

—Yes...different fathers. But I never considered him a
alf-brother.

wayne swallowed hard before continuing:

—My brother's voice was there...so soft and clear. It was
 real as when Tom saw the ghost of his brother Ben. My brother
ld me to be careful and to lead my life knowing we'd be together

again. He never mentioned Heaven, but it was as if he was in some kind of heaven he was not supposed to talk about. I can really listen and hear his voice, Ann. I know it was my brother who sent you. Don't you see?

She could see his eyes flaring in the dark. He leaned closer to her. All her life she'd been an atheist and yet now at this moment wanted so much to believe him, despite so many reasons to stay detached and proselytize. She wanted to talk to him about reincarnation and how his brother came here to evolve; and to tell him what she knows about karma and all the important lessons we've all come here to learn. But he's so into the Christian/God thing, his brother the winged angel visiting him from Heaven, sent by an all-powerful Father to comfort him.

She sat up, wanting to leave with him now, though the bed was quite comfortable and warm to her back.

—I think we should go, he said.

On the walk to the Dixieland parking lot, he talked fast, more about his lost brother.

—He wore so much armor...he couldn't feel anything new. Have you ever known anyone who was bi-polar?

—No, but I don't believe it's all about a chemical imbalance either.

He asked her how old she was as they neared her car.

—How old do you think I am? she smiled, relieved to be out of Dixieland.

—I'd say about thirty.

—Close. Thirty-two, she lied. Are you going to follow me?

—You want to know how old I am? he smiled.

—No, she laughed.

He laughed, too, all the way to his car while thinking he could get lucky with this beautiful girl.

It took them about two minutes to reach her dinky
apartment on Haywood, but a few blocks from downtown. When
he crossed her threshold he knew for sure his brother had sent her
to him. Crystals blinked everywhere, from a hundred spaces as she
lit a dozen cinnamon-scented candles throughout the small, main,
sparsely furnished room. When his brother was having a tough
time selling real estate, he heard cinnamon was good for manifesting prosperity, so he gave his brother a pack of cinnamon gum as a
little joke.

—That's cinnamon, he declared to Ann.

She nodded, her long brown ponytail bobbing in the candlelight.

—You don't strike me as someone who has many visitors,
he said.

Her brown eyes knew that was right, but widened a bit into a
lightened playful look when she asked:

—Would you like some tea?

—Yes.

From the dull illumination of her stove's light, he listened to
how quietly she did everything. It was a shy kind of quiet that
didn't want to disturb things: Silverware was placed down gently
without sound; cupboards and drawers were opened and closed
with minimal creaking. Even her long, graceful bare feet moved on
the hardwood floor with the grace and lightness of a cat. He
wanted to ask her a thousand things about her life and family in
Portland, and how it was for a young woman to move across
country alone with no support. Instead:

—You read all three of my books?

—Yes, I really liked them, she said in this animated whisper.
I want to read your next one. When will it be out?

—When I drive down to Winston-Salem in my new motor
home and pick them up...soon.

—But you live in Asheville, right?

—Not for long.

—You're hittin' the road in a motor home?

—Yeah. I wanna do library book signings...get a cabin here and there and do some marketing and writing.

—That's so cool. But don't you have to have a home base?

—I use my sister's address in Phoenix. I've always been a gypsy, so I admit it and keep movin'.

—Dwayne, I really envy that lifestyle. I wish I could do that.

She got up from the other end of the sofa. He watched her full figure glide into the kitchen after the tea. When she returned with both hands carrying cups on saucers, he paid attention to her return to the other end of the brown sofa after soundlessly placing down the tea. The way she tucked both legs under her, her covered knee to him under that long cream-yellow cotton shirt. It was so feminine and yet so powerful, like a healthy cat with brown eyes that tell him she does not speak the monkey mind and bother with small talk.

She was content to sit there, so relaxed and sipping her tea. He noticed her hair down, released from her ponytail; it was so lush and healthy all the way to her lower back. He did not care if she saw him looking at her hair. Just now, she appeared much younger to him.

—Your hair...is incredibly beautiful, he said.

—Thank you, she smiled so matter-of-factly as if she was not at all in need of a compliment to raise her self esteem, for she is quite comfortable in her skin these days.

During this long space of beautiful silence (that was not an awkward pause or a feeling of boredom, rather, a good stillness like you'd get during and after a long nature walk) she broke the stillness:

—How long have you been planning to hit the road in a motor home?

—I'm a gypsy, so it's been pullin' at me since I moved here

—I wish I could do that...just get up and move on.

—Why don't you? he smiled.

She put down her cup without a sound, then folded her arms in front of her and really thought about it before answering:

—It's money. I'd have no way of supporting myself. That's why I envy you. You have a vehicle...your books.

He turned away from her brown eyes, and thought about the last four words, "You have a vehicle." Those were the same words his brother used during their last conversation on the phone. That was the memory that hit so hard. He had told his brother "no" when his brother wanted to market his books for him. Yes, he had turned his back on his brother when he was asking for help. Was that why now he was going out of his way to offer his help? he wondered. Or, was he wanting this young, beautiful creature with her full body on the lonely road with him? Yes.

—I know we don't know each other. I mean, not yet. But, if you want to go with me, I will cover your expenses and pay your way back to wherever you want to go...if and when you want.

He watched her sitting there, looking at the idea and the whirling reasons why and why not with this wan look of disbelief on her lips.

—Just think about it. It's an offer, he smiled.

Look What I Didn't See

The next day, the third of October, was Tom's 100th birthday. Tour buses were coming to Dixieland in droves. People of all ages were flocking to the boyhood home of America's most passionate novelist while Ann Bruin sat in Laura's Restaurant in Hendersonville, some 25 miles south of Asheville, sipping her hot green tea and picking at a cranberry croissant.

She knew she was in big trouble with her boss Scott at Dixieland when she called her manager this morning, telling him she's taking a sick day:

—What?! This is the busiest day of the year! I can't run all the tours myself! Scott railed in disbelief.

Ann thought about how Dwayne should be halfway through his session with Marjorie about four blocks away; Marjorie would be helping him clear core emotional issues buried at the deepest cellular level of his physical/emotional body. Ann's had three sessions with her, getting at these core issues that had been holding her in unwanted habits and nonproductive behavior patterns that kept her from emotional freedom in all of her relationships. And what did she get out of these sessions with Marjorie? That's why she missed work today.

Marjorie's tough fingers on her left hand thumped her new client's thymus repeatedly as her right hand probed and found the nest of negative emotions stored in his belly on his left side, close to his rib cage.

—How long are you going to grieve for the loss of your brother? she demanded in that Southern drawl while probing and thumping.

—I don't know! he cried

—Okay. Breathe. That's it. Do you think you could have saved your brother?

Again, his eyes opened.

—Close your eyes. Quickly, yes or no. Do you think you could have saved your brother?

—No! Yes! Maybe! No! NO!!

Still thumping his thymus, Marjorie brought her right hand up to his chest and, with both hands, began digging into his bare chest above his breast:

—How does that feel, Dwayne? she yelled.

—It hurts!

—That's it! Let go of that anger you hold onto! Are you angry with your brother? she asked.

—YES! he screamed.

Next: Marjorie took hold of Dwayne's right wrist, raised it up, then simulated pounding the side of her leather treatment table with his hand.

—Get it out, Dwayne! NOW!

His right hand whacked the table hard three times while he screamed:

—I'm mad at you, John!!

—For what? Marjorie asked.

—For killing yourself! he raged.

Back to thumping his thymus:

—And why else are you mad at your brother?

—For having Mother find you!! Dwayne screamed as he pounded the table side with the pinky end of his fist. Then, he sobbed, his chest heaving as Marjorie felt for stored emotions just above his boxer shorts up to his rib cage on his left side; then, again he tapped his chest:

—That's better, Dwayne. You're letting go of real bad stuff, hon. Keep breathing from your toes. Good. Take your breath from as deep as you can.

—Anything else you want to say about your brother?

His eyes rolled up to the ceiling, scanning his thoughts and feelings, until:

—No. There's nothing.

—Good.

—You know Ann, who referred me to you?

—Yes.

—I asked her to go on the road with me. I don't know her very well. Do you know any reason why I shouldn't have her go with me?

She nodded no, smiling at her new client's relaxed countenance.

When his session was over they hugged goodbye. She told him how the grief had left his face after he gave her ninety bucks cash.

His body felt naked after unloading all that anger and grief on Marjorie's table. He didn't realize it, but as he walked carefree along Hendersonville's downtown storefronts on his way to Laura's Restaurant, he was in some kind of re-youthing zone—a time when his body was alive and charged with the vigor of a twenty-year-old. Just then: as he stopped to look at a bowling bag in a trophy shop window, his head began spinning faster and faster, painlessly taking him back to a memory so vivid he could not move or open his eyes if he wanted to, for the pictures in his head were so clear that he wanted to see more of this flashback that was 37 years ago:

It was 1964, in the hottest part of July—daytime. Highway 77 South from Woodbury to Wichita, Kansas, was about 350 miles or a five-hour drive back then when the speed limit was 75. It seemed like such a long drive then, and it was rare when Mom took all of us three kids on a long trip together. We were stopped once by the Nebraska Highway patrol—not for speeding, a warning: "You kids stop fighting or you'll cause your mother to get in an ccident."

That warning kept me, age 12, Karen was 10, and little ohnny was 4, all quiet until Wichita; and I know it probably saved ur lives. My mother's name is Linn; her kids were as different as ie colors and shapes of their eyes. I was mature and sullen and ad a Mad Magazine sense of humor. Karen was always over- eight and lazy and had the same sense of humor as I. Johnny was ie baby, the only child from Linn's second marriage; and he was a ead-ringer for the original Curly on *The Three Stooges*: bald- eaded butch haircut, pot belly with bird legs and he had much igger and brighter blue eyes than I.

I never thought of Johnny as a half-brother. Never. I know iat divorces and different fathers never really divide siblings, ecause they are equal in mind, and share evenly the shame, the isidious shame of divorce.

I remember that my mother's nerves were wracked, even efore that drive to Wichita, because she was recently separated om Johnny's father, and fresh out of the courtroom with her 400.00 per month separate maintenance awarded by the judge.

She was in Wichita to see her old boyfriend for a loan.

They watched their mother's gold and white '59 Fairlane ave the bowling alley parking lot. Mom could trust me to watch ie kids and keep them safe. I liked being in control, but I didn't now I liked it at the time. Only Karen knew that.

Johnny's white legs went inside the cool bowling alley first. hat's when I gave my first order of the day to Karen:

—Go get him.

aren ignored the order, but then: she thought about all that ioney, the twenty and ten-dollar bill Mom gave Dwayne for their od and entertainment until she returned. Karen obeyed.

They had the whole place to themselves. It was massive. eventy-two lanes. And air conditioned.

Karen and Johnny watched their big brother carefully put

the big bills in the bill compartment of the black cowhide billfold Dwayne and Karen's father bought Dwayne in Wyoming at Little America.

Behind the long, high counter sat a corpulent pock-marked man of about 30; he ran the whole place when the owner was gone. He appeared annoyed that now he'd have to get up and do something. The man wheezed when he bent down and flipped on a switch that lit up the first twelve alleys and pins, and moved a penumbra shadow that covered the lanes. Johnny thought it looked like Christmas, as he stared at the alleys after hiking up his beige cut-offs, soon ambling like a little ape on bird legs back and forth excitedly from the ball racks to his siblings:

—Dwayne! Dwayne! Can I pick out a ball? he begged in that high-pitched squeal.

—Get yer bowling shoes first! Dwayne returned before asking Karen:

—What size does the bonehead wear?

—I don't know, Karen shrugged, being the least excited of the trio.

All this time: the taciturn attendant was smoking a non-filtered cigarette from his pack that was rolled up into his short-sleeved shirt just below his shoulder; he looked like a cruel sort of man who might say something mean to them if they didn't hurry up

—C'mon, Johnny! Dwayne called out to his brother who was kneeling at the ball rack looking at all the colored balls that were about the size and shape and weight of his own head.

The attendant looked as insolent as any slug in Wichita when Dwayne gave him a ten-dollar bill to pay for the 40-cent shoe rental.

—That the smallest bill ya got? he scowled at Dwayne. Karen stayed behind to hear her brother's reply as Johnny ran for lane 12, because when brother Dwayne was left in charge in public places he usually said something outrageous, then blushed from barrassment when sister Karen tried to top him, for Dwayne and aren were Ben and Pam in *Ledges*. Dwayne smiled so broadly his otruding overbite was all the attendant could see when Dwayne ushed after saying:

—Yeah...thank goodness.

ae man's bovine stare moved over to Karen's big brown eyes hen she quipped in a fake Wichita drawl:

—Dwayne...you got change and dollar bills. You just want ore dollar bills 'cause you like cash in your pocket.

—You liar, Pam! Her brother blushed and walked away th their score sheet.

—Just for that...you keep score, he told Karen.

—I'm not keepin' score, she complained while lumbering ter he brother.

When Karen and Johnny were looking for colorful bowling lls, not paying attention to the weight of the ball, Dwayne barked:

—The red ones are the lightest! Get a red one that fits yer gers!

hen Karen and Johnny argued for their favorite color:

—Get red...or yer dead! The others are too heavy! And n not gonna tell ya again! If I have to tell ya again...NO POP! O CANDY! OKAY? RED! Just do what I tell ya for once!

Yes, but today in the 21st century, Dwayne the man, D. H. ayne the writer, had thought about his actions for those ten ousand hours when he was in charge of his sister and brother. He ought about it often. And, he knows now that he did it all wrong. a boy, he had taught himself that using guilt, force, and putting ar in their hearts had gotten control of the situation, but it was a d and unfair trade that came back as an insidious retribution in e ways he and his family lived their lives later.

Now: he can only take so much responsibility, since he was ll that boy himself in many ways emotionally. Today he is able to show more love and gladness to those close to him. But not that many are close to D. H. Dayne.

He knows he went back to that Wichita bowling alley to remember two moments: one of them was about Johnny. Somewhere in one of those five games they bowled that day, Johnny got hot and managed to roll seven strikes in a row. In a row! And not one other soul was there to see this incredible feat b a four-year-old, except the three of them.

Dwayne remembered how Johnny was so hoarse and excited from celebrating his 7th strike in a row. Karen and Dwayne kept looking at each other in disbelief with upset stomachs from cheering and too much orange pop and potato chips.

And the second thing: Dwayne went outside while Karen and Johnny ate loosemeats and pop. On the gravel landscaping near the front door, Dwayne removed the bills from the billfold his father gave him, and he buried the gift under the gravel beside a light pole; and he said something ceremonial in nature but he couldn't recall what it was. He thought it was about returning, returning to Wichita when he was wealthy, but he couldn't recall exactly.

Then: in the present, a place he most cherished, he stood staring at his reflection in the storefront window. It was now a reflection of how handsome he was. He thought it a trick window like in a clothing store, when they make you see yourself thinner. was the way his mouth relaxed, and the tension in his eyes had vanished. He moved away from his image in the glass and knew that other people would let him know if he had let go of stuff.

Ann. He walked fast, down the sidewalk until he crossed Main. He thought of the ceremony in Riverside Cemetery where h burned his rejections over Tom's grave. Somehow he believed it was all connected to that bowling alley and all those strikes his brother rolled. It was such a miracle to him and Karen then—and till is today when he imagines how slow that red ball was moving own the alley. It was so lucky. And he was always so lucky in ames, I mean really lucky. And now this: his memory has come own to a puddle of salty tears under Marjorie's massage table in Iendersonville.

On his way to Marjorie's he recalled how he was negative bout Hendersonville, because the librarian here returned his books ith a note:

Mr. Dayne, I am returning the books you sent me. I doubt very 1uch that anyone in my library would want to read them."

But now, after Marjorie, he has that old spark of the super alesman in his step, wishing he had a dozen books riding his hip, e'd soon sell every gawd-damn one of 'em to the small businesses ere and show that librarian a thing or two, he chuckled to himself.

A block away from Ann, he thought the spinning back in me was somehow related to his writing and who he really is, as 1e day in Wichita when his mother went there to get money from a vealthy boyfriend so her family was not so strapped. Did I want vealth so I could take care of my mother? he asked himself, as he 100k his head no, while he was able to see that image of the empty illfold he ceremoniously buried outside the bowling alley over 30 ears ago.

When he reached Laura's, Ann saw he had a good session ith Marjorie. He sat across from her.

—You look great, she smiled.

—She's terrific. She really goes after it...that's for sure.

—Yes, she does.

Ie picked up her tab on the table and told her he wanted her to see is new home.

Outside Laura's, he wanted so much to put his hand into Ann's hand, but he didn't feel she would be receptive to that— erhaps because he was old enough to be her father. But worse han that: he looked old enough to be her father, even after

Marjorie. Last night, before drifting off to sleep, alone on Ann's sofa, he spent time thinking about going to her in her room, but he did not. The excitement of a younger woman without kids, never married, or other negative baggage, was a turn-on for him, but it was the way she helped him experience Marjorie and didn't ask about any details on the way to Lawn Boy or on the drive to the RV dealer that told him volumes of what she would be like as a road companion. Could Ann Bruin be the perfect gypsy girl to live happily on the road with him?, he wondered. It seemed too easy. He always thought he'd find "her" while in the throes of his travels. Perhaps she'd be at one of his book signings; or, he would meet her working as a waitress in some obscure café in the Midwest.

Whenever he met "her," at that instant, she would take his hand in hers and lead him to manifest prosperity for them. She would discover the lost billfold from Wyoming's Little America, saving a part of his lost brother who was so lucky in games. That was a big blunder he made in his last novel *Missouri Madness*; he had mistakenly finished it without working it through. He had written that book for the money, when his brother was plotting his death by his own hand. WY.

Dwayne's new home is a 30-foot Winnebago Adventurer, silver with white trim. What clinched the sale: Dwayne told the sales rep he'd be pulling his car, so the man gave Dwayne a deal on a car trailer, and had it all hitched up for him so the writer could drive off in his new home, pulling Lawn Boy.

When driving away from the RV dealer lot, he told Ann he could put her car on the trailer; that way she could leave in her car when she wanted. That appealed to her. He said that he could park Lawn Boy on his printer's vast parking lot in Winston-Salem. No problem. In other words: he really wanted Ann to go on the road with him. It wasn't a sexual thing, but, it was.

Ann moved up to the front passenger seat after exploring

he back bedroom, and how the bed felt under her while moving.

—I have a name for him, Dwayne stated.

—Him? she queried.

—Yes, his name is Traveller. He has to have a man's name.

—Why?

—I don't know. Protection, maybe. Who knows? All my vehicles have had masculine names.

She smiled as her eyes roamed to the back and front. Never did she have an apartment furnished this nicely, with a brown leather recliner and matching leather hide-a-bed. And two TVs, one in the bedroom and one big screen up front above the windshield. Then, as her eyes roamed over the hills on the horizon, he wanted to tell her why he named his motor home Traveller, but he stopped himself. It was his Aunt Cleone, who told his mother that they were related to Virginia's Robert E. lee on Cleone's maternal side. That was a few weeks before Cleone died, about eight years ago. Dwayne wanted to ask his aunt why she didn't reveal this earlier in his life, for he had been an ardent fan of General Lee for many years. (Who knows what kind of confidence that might've instilled in a struggling writer who could use all the help he could get?) Even when his brother John and he played endless games of backgammon, he was Lee and John was Grant. Instead, he asked Ann:

—Lunch to celebrate Traveller at the Grove Park Inn?

She smiled.

He liked the way Traveller handled the winding road that was shaded by tall Carolina pines, and he was impressed by the way Ann was so quietly aware of her surroundings; it was as if she was really getting the feel for what it would be like to be on the road in Traveller.

The silence was beautiful, as the Adventurer by Winnebago made the sinuous web of curves with ease and comfort, as if riding in a Lincoln. But more thoughts kept coming to him about his brother. All of those thoughts were about things he knew she would listen to with interest, but it would distract them from this peaceful ride together. After all, he was not looking for a sounding board or a 30-year-old woman to seduce; he was looking for a woman to distract him from all those lonely nights ahead when he'd surely be ruminating about his brother, and the thousand times he'd have to tell his mind to "stop it" and change his thought pattern.

Alone would be hard, he knew. A man cannot grow when alone all the time. Could she be a soul mate, sent here to teach me a lesson or many lessons? he wondered, as she tucked her square little leather purse under Traveller's passenger seat while he parked in an area marked for buses in the massive network of parking spaces two hundred yards from the stately Grove Park Inn.

—I love that orange trim, she said, as they walked toward the massive hotel with its chocolate brown stones glistening in the early-autumn sunlight.

—You talk about places loaded with history. Imagine all the interesting people who've stayed here, he said.
She smiled that contented way she always looked, as they admired the hotel's immense power until they were in the loop of the young men who made up the concierge. Their long-sleeved white shirts were clean and impressive, their faces poised to serve vs. the usual glumness of today's youth giving lousy service.

When they entered the hotel's grand lobby, they clicked on simultaneously that today is Tom's birthday. The main room was saturated with early 20th century furnishings from when Tom must've been here in his boyhood and later when he visited after his first book was so popular.

They strolled over to one of the huge fireplaces that was empty, blackened from many fires.

—Ya know what sounds good? Dwayne said.

—What?

—Some hot apple cider on the terrace.

he smiled as he continued:

—It's too cool for lunch on the terrace. Hot cider sounds ood. Then lunch inside.

They were alone on the expansive terrace that overlooked ie Blue Ridge in front of the new spa under construction. Their ugs of cider steamed upward in the frosty October air. They were alf-turned to the panoply of autumn's million trees lush to the orizon when she said without turning to him:

—I'm considering going with you. But not as your lover. o you probably won't want me along. I can understand that. he moved her brown eyes to the spa area; she could feel his eyes n her when he told her:

—I enjoy your company. You're probably right. I would et frustrated being so close to you in Traveller. But, if you want o get away for a week or two...I could handle that. I'll be in 'irginia, so you wouldn't have far to drive if you come back to sheville.

—Where in Virginia?

—Virginia Beach, first. Then Williamsburg, Fredericks-urg and Richmond. he thought about it, again turning to the view while sipping her ider.

—I'm leaving in two days, the morning of the fifth. My ent's paid till the fifth. That might not be enough time for you, he aid.

—I'll let you know tomorrow, she said.

—Okay...but if you decide to go, bring only clothing, 'cause travel light. No extra stuff or...you know.

—Yeah, okay, she smiled. he didn't want to mention the fact she moved here with only a ack seat full of clothes.

After lunch, they went to his cabin in Oteen. He loaded

some things into Traveller, mostly his valuable writing collection that consisted of boxed copies and originals of his many scripts and novels. Ann was the only person he knew in Asheville who had read his three titles. As she helped him load some of his things, they talked:

     —So, your fourth book is ready at your printer in Winston-Salem...and you're picking them up on your way to Virginia?

     —Right.

     —How many copies did you say you had printed?

     —Five thousand.

     —And you're going to haul them with you?

     —Yeah. It's a few hundred pounds over a ton. I'll be sellin' 'em at libraries along the way.

     —Only libraries?

     —Mostly. I can't make a living with retail. Libraries are my best outlet. Bookstores want them on consignment or return them if they don't sell. They return too many. I hate that. I believe I can sell some books at library book signings.

     —Seems like the hard way.

After shoving another box into Traveller's storage area, he answered:

     —No, the hard way is to do nothing and work some dead-end job I hate.

     —You have an agent?

     —No. Don't want one or need one.

She followed him into his cabin as he talked:

     —Marketing my own books this way may seem like the hard way, but it's not. Waiting and waiting to be validated by that one good reader who wants to publish or represent you, that's the hard way. This way, I'm getting read and I feel like I have readers who want me to keep writing.

     —Uh huh. You need to change the font. Your first two books are hard to read. *Missouri Madness* is easier to read, though e stories are very interesting.

    —My books are sold out. I'm not printing any of my first ree titles again. I'll live off my new book.

ıst before she sat down on his sofa, he asked her if she'd ever been Tom's cabin in Oteen?

    —The one he stayed in after the heat cooled from *Angel*?

    —Yeah. We can walk there from here.

    It was sunset when they could see the cabin a few hundred ırds away. They had talked the entire trek of maybe two miles ıd were there before they knew it. He talked about his sister aren and how she became interested in astrology when she had to et a wheelchair. "The chair," as Karen referred to it cynically, she ımed Perry. Dwayne laughed when he told Ann how he used to ıll his sister Perry years before because she argued like an attorney ıd the fact that she was over a hundred pounds over-weight. And e went on how he called Karen Ironsides from Raymond Burr's V show after she got her wheelchair. Ann had no clue who Perry Iason was. Dwayne said that when his sister e-mailed him, she'd ırite: "oh, we're fine. Perry and I are just sittin' around watchin' oller Derby on the tube." Dwayne would describe Karen's herubic face and big brown eyes lighting up when she laughed; and ow she was the most positive person he ever met in his life, all ecause of the pain she lives with; she uses humor to mitigate that ain.

    Dwayne then rambled on about his sister's recent interest in arot Cards. He was surprised when Ann talked about the Tarot ecks "Golden Dawn," "Tree of Life," and "The Witch's Tarot." Ie told Ann how he heard about people calling the tarot an occult, ıd that Karen knew her Bible and just did tarot for fun. Then Ann ıld Dwayne that people who consider the Bible as the be-all— ıd-all of spirituality is a mistake, and that people who do that do ot worship God. They worship a book, and value letters more than meaning and become judgmental of others, and hypocritical in their lives. She went on to say how those people build up their own egos and forget what true compassion is all about. She said that compassion in the spiritual person is a natural act. Compassion in the religious person is done out of duty to authority, and recognition by others of the services performed.

Tarot's Kabbalah, Ann explained, is not about your love life or telling your future; it's about the correction of the inner self so one can build a better, more productive life.

Dwayne asked her how she knew so much about Tarot Cards. She said her ex-boyfriend's mother played with the cards.

Dwayne told her about his one good reader in Grey, Maine. Ann thought that was an act of God, perhaps his way to become a writer/in.

Then he told her about this sidereal chart his sister was working on, a chart that listed his best places to be according to his birth time and place compared to several different categories: love, prosperity, health, family, friendship, mystery, past life, home, and others.

She thought it interesting if Karen could match his library book signings with such a chart, to make a life as interesting as possible. Ann had heard of such a chart in Portland, but never knew anyone who actually followed it around the country.

At Tom's cabin: Dwayne told Ann he knew the caretaker who lived nearby, and that he could get the key from him. Ann made a joke about going in through an open window; they laughed about it until the caretaker's door opened.

When they walked away with the key, Ann pointed to a bunch of fuchsia-colored flowers growing alone next to an old, rusty push lawnmower parked against the cabin. Dwayne had no clue what kind of flower it was either. He veered away from her and plucked one of them from the earth, handing it to her after smelling its sweet petals covered with velvet/white hairs. She put the flower to her lips, and closed her eyes when she inhaled its fragrance. Then, from her pocket, she took out a vile of essential oil, removed its cap and swirled it in a figure eight rising to her nostrils, taking in deeply the sweet aroma before handing it to Dwayne.

—What is it?

—Joy, she smiled, her eyes dreamy from the intoxicating/ sweet oil composed of lemon, rose, rosewood, geranium and chamomile.

—Aromatherapy, he smiled. I wonder what it would be like if you spent all day breathing in this...joy. What would happen?

—If your mind was really into feeling joy, you'd feel pretty good, I imagine.

It was the way she laughed when she said that, so tickled by the joy the oil gave her, as if programmed by a thousand such meditations; it made him ask her if she meditated or ever had.

—Yes, I do, every morning.

—You would be good for me on the road. Even if for only a week or two. You'd get me back into good habits.

She unlocked the cabin door after taking the key from him, wanting to step inside first. It was getting dark fast. A framed photo of Tom was centered above the mantle. Dwayne demonstrated how tall Tom was by raising his elbow unable to reach the ledge of the mantle.

Ann brushed her hand over the top of the table where Tom wrote in front of the fireplace. She said:

—I've seen photos of him writing at this table. When do you write, Dwayne?

He flinched a bit, caught off guard; her quick eye caught him staring at the rhythm of her full-bodied thighs and hips in slight motion against the table.

—I write in restaurants, mostly...after a meal. I like to be in a public place when I write the first two drafts. But at night I type the final draft at home.

Her step was lithe as she peeked in at the unfurnished bedroom and kitchen. He thought about how he should keep his mouth shut and not hound her about going on the road. No more, he vowed.

On the narrow path near his cabin, it was already dark when he broke his vow to himself after asking her if he could smell the vile of joy:

—So, do you know yet if you can hit the road?

—I have to talk to the director at the library first and see if I can have a leave of absence.

—That's smart. What about Dixieland?

—Same thing. Today was the busiest day of the year at Dixieland. I don't think they appreciated me playing hookie.

As they neared Dwayne's cabin, she told him she had a month-to-month lease at her apartment and could easily be out with her things in a few hours if she could go. Then: she surprised him:

—You don't have to take me home in Traveller. I might as well stay the night here. That is...if you don't mind.

—Oh, no...are you kidding? That'll be great.

For Dwayne, it was fun and exciting loading his things from the cabin into Traveller. They talked the whole time; it seemed that time flew by so fast he couldn't remember where he put half his things in his new Adventurer.

Later into the night, they sat in Traveller drinking wine from a bottle of red Merlot from the Biltmore Estate he had been saving for a special occasion; this was as special as it gets for him—when an attractive woman is alone with him and listening to his every word.

They sat across from each other at the cushioned table with

their backs against Traveller's expandable wall. She asked him:

—Have you been dating much?

He laughed quietly before saying:

—I don't know what it is...but I'm in my mid-40s and I don't care about that anymore. I guess if I did, I wouldn't be hittin' the road with a motor home. How 'bout you?

—Not since I moved to Asheville.

—What about before, in Oregon?

—Oh, I had a boyfriend, but it was mostly physical—nothing really of any substance.

—What is substance for you?

—A connection. More than spiritual. A knowing that together you are more than you could be alone.

—Uh huh, he yawned, and told her he would sleep in Traveller so she could have his bed in the cabin.

—Oh, no, she insisted. I'll sleep here. I'd like to test it out and see how I like it.

—Okay, he smiled, wishing they could test it together.

He gave her a comforter and a pillow and told her she's the first person to sleep in Traveller. He had about everything loaded in his new home. He told her he'd treat her to a big breakfast downtown tomorrow before going over to her apartment.

He laid under his cracked-open bedroom window, restless, wanting her with him now on his last night in Asheville. He wanted to tell her how alive and young he feels when he's with her, and how the energy he had put into marketing his books was exacting a toll on his ability to market himself to any available women. And how he just knew and felt his chances diminished, season after season, to find a woman who is independent and good for him.

And he wanted to press Ann's full body to his; and spoil her by bathing her in his independence on the road. By showing her how to be independent and removed from the trappings of being taken-care-of, she would then see she had no more use for the younger men who only take from her.

And with her touch, she would melt this anger he believed the universe or God was keeping him trapped in. The same anger Marjorie had felt in his belly, a gnawing, creeping kind of rage that suspended his aliveness because he had not learned the gawd-damned festering lessons related to his brother's suicide. Would he spend his entire life thinking of this terrible act that made him drip long strands of slobbering tears onto Marjorie's floor, that made him punch walls and doors and furniture during dry spells while marketing his self-published books—books that were not good enough for the real publishing world, an alien/specious world that could validate him and make him a writer/in.

Then: he imagined her riding in Traveller, shotgun, her long brown lustrous hair alive in the breeze on America's back roads and side roads he knew as well as anyone. The places: parking areas off the beaten path where they would make love and have picnics staring at nature, eating healthy foods they carried in Traveller; lakes in Minnesota and North Dakota that were clear and cold with choppy waves from the cold winds that blew down from Canada; and those ten thousand little towns he would walk with her, along Main Street, holding hands, smiling at every stranger, letting everyone know that they are much happier and far better people when together—yet always independent.

He imagined sharing the endless vistas of the Southwest in Flagstaff, Payson, Santa Fe, Show Low. But always: there were places like Show Low, that reminded him of his brother. His brother had taken him there a year before his death. And how now Dwayne knew it was more important than ever for him to find that special woman, a soul mate, a "good woman" John called her. A woman like Ann Bruin. If Dwayne could just keep a "good woman's" love, he could justify a thousand moves when he was a gypsy; and he could diminish some of the terribleness of his brother's death along with some of the final haunting words his brother spoke to him:

—I always thought we'd live together on my land near The Superstitions.

John had said that they were so alike and likely to never marry; they would grow old together because they probably would never find a good woman.

Oh, how he wanted to be straight-on with Ann and get right to the heart of things he felt about her. This anxiousness to love her would have to be toned down, or she'd run.

Before he went to sleep, he thought about John Candy in his screenplay *Wayne*, and a scene where he left off before:

Chris Rea's song *Fool, If You Think It's Over* begins as the blistering Texas morning sun beats down on Rusty, Wayne's rusted-out gold '68 Olds that is out of gas on the shoulder of a lonely stretch of highway near Brownsville. Rusty was Wayne's high school graduation present 20 years ago, as we see Wayne's 20-year high school reunion letter on Rusty's dashboard. Rusty has mis-matched bald tires, one is a donut tire; a clothes hanger waves as a makeshift radio antenna in the Texas wind.

Wayne wakes up on Rusty's front seat wearing the same hanky with cucumber slices covering his eyes. Wayne's clothes are piled on Rusty's back seat as he removes the hanky while sweating heavily; his eyes are burning and his vision is blurred from the pesticides in the cucumber.

—My eyes! I can't see, Rusty! I'm blind here!

Wayne grabs a jug of water and dabs water from his palm into his eyes, complaining to Rusty:

—Cucumbers are s'pose to be good for ya!

His eyes are swollen shut; he can barely see while opening his driver-side door from the outside. When he opens Rusty's trunk we can see a cardboard sign in Rusty's back window that reads: "Out of Gas." He talks to his car while getting his empty gas can

-79-

from the trunk:

    —You know the routine. Wait here.
Wayne closes the trunk and pats it goodbye as if a friend.

    Later: Wayne, his eyes yet swollen and barely able to see, is
sweating profusely while walking along the hot shoulder with no
traffic in sight from either direction on the shimmering highway.

    —Good thing I can still breathe, he mumbles good-
naturedly.

    Later: Wayne's curled up on his belly, covering his face
with his hands while on the desert ground waiting out a dust storm
that's blacked out everything...except his memory. As the wind and
dust howl around him, we go to Wayne's flashback of 20 years
ago:

    It's a summer night in 1968 in Dekalb, Illinois. Eighteen-
year-old Wayne and his high school sweetheart Bonnie, also 18, are
parked in his new car (Rusty) at their favorite parking spot under a
big oak tree in the country. After they've made love on Rusty's
back seat, they lie together, under a sheet on a pillow, talking:

    —Wayne, what are you going to do with your life?

    —I don't know. Join the Marines, maybe. They're lookin'
for a few good men, he chuckled.

    —You'd go to Viet Nam, Wayne. Go to college. I don't
want you to go in the Marines.

    —I've gotta do somethin'. Maybe I'll join the Navy, like
my dad.

    —You can work in my dad's store. You might not get
drafted.

    —Bonnie, my lottery number is 16.

    —You've got flat feet. My dad said they won't draft you if
you have flat feet.

    —Oh, yeah, I'll just stay in yer dad's store on my flat feet
all day...while all my buddies serve their country.

    —What buddies?

—Well, you know, guys–the guys over there.

—Oh, Wayne, I don't want you to go over there. You might not come back to me, she cried.

—Okay, okay, don't cry, sweetie. I'll go in the Navy. That's safer.

As he holds Bonnie, we fade out to:

INT - PATROL GUNBOAT HELM - NIGHT

Wayne, in Navy- issued work clothes, is sweating while on the helm as the barrel of a 8" gun is pointed at the helm; a shell is dangerously lodged in the gun turret. As officers chat behind Wayne:

—Sir, isn't it time for me to be relieved, sir?

Later that night: Wayne's cramped on the top bunk under his reading light, writing a letter home to Bonnie. We hear his voice reading the letter as he continues writing to her:

—Hi, sweetie! I don't want you to worry...but I almost got blown to smithereens a while a go when a live round got lodged in a gun turret. I somehow knew I'd be okay. I kept thinking about you and how much I love and miss you. I can't wait to see you on my next leave. I don't mean to worry you, but telling you this means something. Do I want you to worry about me? Feel sorry for me? Or, do I want you to think I am some brave kind of soldier boy so you will wait for me? As if I had risked myself for my country, when, in fact, I nearly shit my pants from tension and fear for my life...and did not do a gawd-damn thing about the whole situation. So don't worry about me, baby. Just wait for me to return to you. Love, Wayne.

P.S. Again, I'm sorry about being a jerk at the truck stop.

At that same moment, when Wayne is waiting for the Texas dust storm to blow away:

Wayne's high school sweetheart Bonnie is sitting on her bed

reading the end of the same letter Wayne wrote her nearly 20 years ago. She returns Wayne's letter to the storage box beside her. Bonnie then lies back on her bed thinking back to her flashback:

INT - TRUCK STOP CAFÉ - NIGHT

Young Wayne and Bonnie sit across from each other holding hands at a table booth late at night in a truck stop café. Wayne's in civilian clothes, on leave from boot camp near Christmastime. He's running out of leave time as he stares dreamily at Bonnie and says:

 —I wish I could freeze time and just look at you.

Bonnie's eyes start to tear. They squeeze hands.

 —Wayne, I always miss you so much.

 —Will you wait for me? he asks.

She starts to cry.

 —Does that mean no? he chuckles.

Bonnie laughs, answering his question:

 —You know I'm yours, Wayne.

 —Since this is our last night before I go back, can you stay over at my place? he asks with hopeful eyes.

She nods yes, squeezing his hand. Wayne picks up his tab from the table and follows Bonnie to the register area where Nick, a high school classmate who Wayne doesn't like, begins chatting with Bonnie. After Wayne pays his bill, he turns to Nick and in a fit of jealousy:

 —Hey, Nick, you still a dick?

Wayne pushes Nick into the jukebox. Bonnie's upset with Wayne's behavior:

 —Wayne! What's wrong with you?

END OF BONNIE'S FLASHBACK

We return to haggard Wayne walking on the hot Texas shoulder after the dust storm. He's closing in on a truck stop at an isolated exit with his empty gas can.

At the gas pump he pulls his empty front pants pockets

side out. Not a dime to his name. He places his gas can near the
gas pump and eyes the soda vending machines near the front
entrance. He walks past the soda machines.

Inside the truck stop, truckers are lined up to pay for their
fuel.

In the truck stop restroom: Wayne is soaking his head in
cold water in one of the basins. After he cleans up a bit, he exits
the restroom and stops at a bulletin board. He reads an 8-1/2 x 11
piece of paper that's titled "ARE YOU TIRED?" in bold/printed
letters. It's a joke about the population of the U. S. being 250
million: 10 million of them working for the government; 1.2 million
for the Post Office; 2.1 million on welfare; 5 million unemployed;
.2 million illegal aliens; 1.8 million in mental hospitals; 2 million in
prison; on and on until: "That leaves you and me, and, brother, I'm
gettin' tired of doin' everything myself."

Wayne laughs out loud, cracking open his dry lips in several places.
Then: he gets an idea: he looks around to see if anyone is looking
his way. He removes the saying from the bulletin board, unnoticed.

Soon, he's getting copies made in the truck stop office and
selling copies for two bucks a copy or three copies for five bucks to
laughing truckers and waitresses.

Later: Wayne is dropped off with his gas can by a trucker
who bought one of his copies of the joke. Wayne has more energy
now as he hurries over to Rusty and begins pouring the gas into
Rusty's tank:

—I got gas and twenty bucks! Don't ask me how! It's a
funny story! he laughs, saving a little gas for Rusty's carburetor:

—I gotta fun way to pay our way now! No more pop
machine scams for us, boy! Laughs for cash! I got my best price
figured at two bucks a copy! Three for five bucks! I made twenty
bucks in a half-hour, Rusty!

Ann had been thinking about how she was born to love him.

She knew at the exact moment when he fell asleep. She felt Traveller's bedroom was not stifling at all, and could see herself spending long hours here. She closed her eyes and listened to her monkey mind's chatter loaded with fear:

—This is so good. A golden chance to act. Do not sleep now. Stay awake, Ann.

She went back to that moment on the terrace at the Grove Park Inn when she felt him looking at her breasts when he thought she wasn't looking. A man so sensitive surely knows that a conscious woman knows when she's being looked over. It didn't really bother her...because she was flattered.

Ann was awake when the Libra half-moon bathed in Carolina darkness on the new day's third hour. It was then that she made her move. It would be a surprise for him, so she made hardly a sound, leaving her hard-heeled shoes at the foot of the bed while her heart raced to do this thing that would totally change their lives forever.

The next morning: Dwayne could smell coffee; he thought it coming from the kitchen. Then, he remembered Ann was asleep in Traveller. He thought that perhaps she made coffee in Traveller since the aroma of fresh coffee was coming from his open bedroom window. What a great day, he smiled. He couldn't remember the last time thinking that with a smile on his face before his feet even hit the floor.

When his bed-warmed flesh stepped out into the crisp October morning air: he goose-pimpled, his skin rising and begging to be warm again with this total sclerotic shock of theft and betrayal, then, confusion. Traveller was gone, and Lawn Boy on the trailer—gone, all gone. She just drove away with nearly everything he owned.

While dialing 911 he thought of the possibility that she just couldn't sleep and thus drove over to her place to load Traveller

ith her things and get that done. He hung up on the 911 operator
id said out loud.

—Yeah, that's prob'ly what she did.

So, he waited anxiously as he cleaned out his cabin and
adied to move out his little things left to take with him or throw
ut.

By noon, only his phone remained; it was on the floor in the
ont room, between his legs. He had just talked to the downtown
sheville librarian where Ann worked. The library director would
it give out any information about Ann Bruin, or even verify if
iat was really her name. He thought about calling his sister
aren, because she would be able to get any information from the
irary here.

It was ten miles to Ann's apartment from his cabin. He
illed a cab and left his phone plugged in, not [wanting] to tell his
ndlord anything yet, for Dwayne told him he'd be moved out by
ve.

All the way across town in his cab ride he kept thinking how
ie keys to Lawn Boy were on the same key ring with the motor
ime's keys that he left in Traveller's ignition.

—She'll be there, he told himself.

She wasn't. Traveller and the trailer and her car—gone.
awn Boy was left in front of her apartment with the key left in the
nition. At least he could drive to the police station. But first:
ven though her apartment was empty and her landlord had no clue
ie'd left, Dwayne gave her the benefit of doubt and drove back to
s cabin in case she was on her way in Traveller with her car on the
ailer. After all, he did offer to take her car.

Again: no sign of her at his cabin. He called the cops; they
ere on their way over to file a report on the stolen vehicle.

—Could she have really ripped me off? he kept asking
mself, now, more worried about all his belongings in Traveller,
pecially his original writings.

Dwayne had given the police officer Ann's landlord's name and her places of employment. He felt pretty stupid after the law left. All he had to his name was his phone, shaving kit, and a few odds and ends that included a roll of toilet paper. The policeman told him that he'd get Traveller back, that it's pretty hard to hide a motor home for long. He felt better after he called his insurance company; they told him he was covered against theft, even all his belongings.

—But what about all my writing? he kept asking. I can't replace that.

His landlord let him stay that night in the cabin, and his printer was notified that he'd be down to pick up his books in a day or two in a U-Haul truck.

That night, he paced inside the cabin, deciding to keep his phone connected until this was over. The outlines of his rejection notices on his wall were more obvious under the ceiling light.

He couldn't go to sleep; so, he walked for the Wolfe cabin he visited with Ann, not sure he'd make it all the way there. He felt like letting out some agonal cry to break up this clot of burbly phlegm at the base of his tongue. The later it became, a half moon shone vanilla bright and was dropping into the hills. A freight train shunting down by the river reminded him of Harvey, his character in *The Paper Man* and Floyd's alter ego and sensitive side that now tried to calm his mind by telling him he can learn a lesson from this and become stronger, even write about it:

That thought: "He could write about it," drove away the negative thoughts of how he should've known that a beautiful woman, a young one, especially, wouldn't be interested in him. He was too old for her (another sign from *The Paper Man*). She saw she could use you, because you were so desperate to have her along. You sap! Wake up...you frigin' dummy!

—Stop it! he ordered his mind.

Then: he stopped in his tracks, listening to his breath; until he heard familiar voice, the raspy excited voice of his dead brother. He rocked his head from side to side unable to make out the words that appeared to come from above his head. He could only make out the words "Virginia Beach."

—What about Virginia Beach? he asked the wraith while looking up into the black ink sky.

Nothing more came. He turned and headed back for his cabin.

On his return walk, he was taken over again by John Candy, recalling his mind playing scenes from his original screenplay *Wayne*. And that silly saying, "Are you tired?" He questioned why he would think of that "joke" before he went to sleep last night.

—The joke's on me. All over me, he thought. And after he lined me up with Marjorie. Marjorie. She may know things about her if the cops don't find her. Yeah...Marjorie.

The thought of Marjorie held him, until: he was beginning to see a stored memory, the memory of his first near-death experience. It was the exact same feeling of spinning back in time without dizziness. And, like when he re-visited the Wichita bowling alley from the storefront window in Hendersonville after Marjorie's treatment—he was in Wichita again, not even feeling the cold Oteen cement road under his knees on that dark dead-end road that led to Tom's cabin.

There was a big desire to see this terrible thing again, in order to be free of it. So...he was there:

In 1959, in Wichita, Kansas, it was just five-year-old Dwayne and three-year-old Karen; his brother John would not be born for three years. Their mother was out of town on a hunting expedition in Canada with her wealthy boyfriend, who was this big oil man from Texas.

Verla was their babysitter. They were staying in Verla's dark brick, one-story home with her eight-year-old son Glenn and Verla's beautiful seventeen-year-old daughter Trudy. Verla was this squat, Quaker-looking woman who talked fast and stammered like Porky Pig when she got excited or upset. Verla looked like a human fire hydrant who was always bursting with this fountain of dither. Her kids never took her seriously, at all. Whenever she got mad at them, they'd ignore her or laugh at her.

Quiet little Dwayne, so well-mannered and in awe of Verla, was yet coping with his parents' divorce. Dwayne could now see that he was fearful of the way Verla's kids treated her. And Karen was a blur to him then. But not that maroon '47 Plymouth that was parked along the curb in front of Verla's house. He can now see so clearly: it's wide body, so much chrome, so heavy looking, and it was shining in that intense Wichita summer sun.

Glenn had hopped onto the back bumper because his mother was going to park her car in the driveway so the boys could wash it for fifty cents each. Dwayne was coaxed by the older boy Glenn as Verla came storming out from her front door. It happened so fast, yet in slow motion: Dwayne had fallen off the rear bumper on the driver's side under the rear tire. He was told later that Glenn screamed, "You ran over Dwayne!" Verla panicked (which didn't take much) and clutched the car forward; the second time she rolled the tire over Dwayne's supple lower back. The neighbor lady watering her lawn across the road fainted into her bed of 4-inch yellow/lime mums.

Back to Now: As he walked toward his cabin, his breath held from the memory of his compressed lungs, without warning: he crapped his pants just as he did when Verla ran over him twice nearly forty years ago.

For a mile, he sauntered like a bow-legged penguin, or, more like an old man who just filled his drawers. He laughed out loud as he passed people cleaning their vehicles at the self-service car wash, for he imagined dropping his pants and using the hand-held spray nozzle on his ass and boxers, but his arms weren't long enough—so he kept jet-spraying every place but the target.

Then, he was laughing as he thought of poor Verla stammering and nearly out of her mind when she carried him inside to her bedroom floor and changed his pants like a baby before driving him to the hospital when he could only breathe those little spasms of air into his compressed lungs.

In the hospital emergency room they put him on his stomach, cut his shirt away from his back; that's when Verla fainted: when she saw the "X" tire impression tracks imprinted on little Dwayne's back.

On his tire path to his cabin he continued to laugh at his predicament and if someone crossed his path now. Then, he stopped laughing, his face now henna colored from the moonlight and blushing blood. He thought about how his messy accident behind him had taken his mind off Traveller and Ann; and then he compared his messy accident to Traveller and how he'd be hauling his shit around America till it was dumped. And he knew he hadn't written a word since he met Ann in Ben's room; and it really felt good to take a break from that daily habit.

—Could that be good for me? he wondered.

Something made him think and laugh at the joke his sister Karen made in Arizona. She told Dwayne that since her brother had this wry sense of humor: he ought to print on the cover of his next book to amuse his readers: "Over one billion readers." Then, in very small print, like the size of print you see on insurance premiums or credit card terms, she said to put in parenthesis (in China).

He laughed all the way to his cabin with his pants filled with shit and his legs bowed as if he had rickets.

In the shower, after tossing his underwear in the garbage can, he heard his brother's voice again.

This time he made out his brother's instructions to see Edgar in Virginia Beach.

—Edgar Cayce? he asked the shower ceiling.

-89-

No answer.

Late into that night he thought about why his brother's voice was telling him to see Edgar Cayce, the sleeping prophet who died with a legacy of healing thousands of people while in a trance. Dwayne had told his brother about Edgar, but then his brother wasn't interested, it seemed, not at all inquisitive, about the miracles Edgar performed.

—Am I going mad? Making up my brother's voice, sending me on some wild goose chase?

The next morning was filled with phone calls to the police, yielding no sign of Ann or Traveller. Dwayne got a cell phone but kept his cabin phone on after calling Karen and giving her Ann's name to see just what she could find out from the library.

Then he drove his car over to Ann's empty apartment; still, no sign of her. Then: he drove over to the library and Dixieland—nothing.

Then, the hardest thing: leaving Asheville for Winston-Salem in a Budget rental truck pulling Lawn Boy on a trailer after closing out his cabin.

Yes, Dwayne Dayne had learned after his brother's death that it's important to live in a zone of serendipity and "to see" those positive things that can result from a negative.

Driving away from his printer with his five thousand copies of his new book, he thought about something librarians who carried his first three books had been telling him over and over. He would try it at the Winston-Salem Public Library, which bought ten copies each of his three titles for the main library and its nine branches. That was serendipity.

Then, it came to him, in some delicate tone, he was told how he should haul his new books back to Asheville, store them by the month, since surely he would be able to get Traveller and his things when Ann was caught and returned to Asheville.

—God, that's it! I can't be drivin' around the country in a frigin' rental truck! This way I can fill my car with books, travel light, and try this new formula on my libraries! Serendipity!

D. H. Dayne was confident when he entered the Winston-Salem Public Library on Highland Avenue with ten copies of his new book, hot off the press, riding on both hands against his slight hummocky belly. He went straight to the reference desk, the place to go if you want any information regarding adult circulation.

—Is Mark in?

—I'm Mark.

—Mark, I'm D. H Dayne from Asheville.

Dwayne paused to see if Mark remembered him. He didn't; he continued:

—You bought my first three books from me over the phone: *Ledges, The Paper Man,* and *Missouri Madness.*

—Oh, yeah, Mark remembered.

—How are they circing? the writer asked.

Mark turned his computer screen to himself and laughed when he saw Dayne's fingers crossed on his countertop. Mark was in a good mood because there were no patrons waiting behind Dwayne.

—Thank God there's no turnipseeds around, Dwayne muttered to himself, a name he called anybody who was at the wrong place at the wrong time; Turnipseed was the name of the poor sap who pulled out in front of James Dean's car, causing the speeding actor's fatal crash.

—I always like to know how my books are circing, Dwayne smiled, putting his new books on the counter before continuing:

—I hear they're doin' okay. At least at most libraries they are. Of course, I could be wrong about your branches.

Mark scanned the screen:

—Eight times in East Winston.

—Which book?

-91-

—*Ledges*, Mark said.

—How 'bout *The Paper Man*?

—Six circs. Nine for *Missouri Madness*.

—That's not bad, the writer said.

Mark checked two other branches: Lewisville and Reynolds Manor, which had pretty much the same numbers.

—Not bad for an unknown, huh Mark?

—Yeah...that's pretty good.

Dwayne knew this was no time to be humble; it's now time to take over and shine:

—Hot off the press...it's my first title in my new series—*Shy Ann*. Hoping I can leave these ten copies with you...and you can send me a p.o.

—I'll call up to acquisitions and get a p.o. now.

—Great. Ten copies?

—Yes.

—There's something else I want to talk to you about, Dwayne said while signing his books. My sister Karen is a librarian in Arizona. She's always tellin' me how libraries always need to raise money. Well, she said that if you put up a sign that says "donations appreciated" with a smiling face, you could put one next to the book and video return slots over there. People could throw their loose change in the slot or you could use one of those five-gallon water jugs so they couldn't get their hands inside it.

—They'd just walk off with it, Mark snorted.

—Yeah, you'd have to secure it somehow. My sister told me that only fifty-eight cents per person in this country is given to public libraries. I just think it's a great idea you can pass on to the director, Mark.

Mark was smiling, then said he didn't think that would raise money for the library here.

—Ya never know. I know some smaller libraries do it and it works. Who knows?

Mark was looking over the cover of *Shy Ann*:

—Nice cover.

—Thanks.

When Mark flipped the book over and read the back cover, it reminded Dwayne about something painful from his third book *Missouri Madness*: Dwayne's brother John had helped telemarket his script version of *Missouri Madness, Michigan Madness* several years ago. It bombed. People did not want to read a screenplay. They telemarketed the script from Des Moines to residents in Bath, Michigan, the town where the Bath School Disaster happened in 1927.

When Mark opened the front cover of *Shy Ann*:

—I dedicated this book and my last book to my brother. He died about the time *Missouri Madness* was finished. I never got to tell him it was dedicated to him.

Just then: a turnipseed called. Mark answered the phone while Dwayne felt the pain in his belly Marjorie had taught him was the place where family emotions are stored. He knew it was the shame he felt for telling his brother no, turning his brother away when John called him just two weeks before his suicide, begging his older brother to let him market his three books for him.

As Mark rattled on the phone, then, answered a reference question, D. H. Dayne's inner dialogue was loud and hard and so real to him:

—My brother was asking for help and I turned him down. That couldn't have saved him, I know. But I feel the shame and regret for not clearly explaining my reasons to him. You have to move on. He's gone. I know. Stop it! Deliver your frigin' books and get back to Asheville.

On his return drive to Asheville, he thought of his brother's suicide that he didn't see coming; and the fact his brother read his novel *Ledges* shortly before his death. In *Ledges*, Gene's best friend D. J. commits suicide after he thinks Gene has drowned.

—I'm drowning now! Dwayne screamed, pounding the truck's steering wheel.

After thinking of Ann and her chicanery, and the fact that there was no clue it was coming, he focused on the little clues his brother left him. For too many miles Dwayne shook his head saying, "Look what I didn't see."

Until he finally ordered himself to "Stop it!".

By 8:00 P.M. he was closing in on Virginia Beach in Lawn Boy. He spent last night near downtown Asheville in a motel. Lawn Boy's trunk was jammed with ten cases of his new book, as well as ten more cases riding on the back seat of his Hyundai. That gave him 1400 books with 3600 more stored in an Asheville storage locker.

Before heading to Virginia Beach this morning, he stopped in to the Asheville Police Station and nearly crapped his pants, again, when a detective told him Ann was caught in Virginia Beach and being held there until federal authorities could pick her up. The cop told him he could pick up his Winnebago at the Virginia Beach Police Station when he filed charges.

His brother's voice, telling him to go to Edgar in Virginia Beach, was on his mind for the duration of his eight-hour drive to the Virginia coast. Just a coincidence? Perhaps, he thought. But no, this was no coincidence. It only made him realize that time when he was in the New Mexico desert just after his brother's death, on his way to be with his mother and Karen, when he heard his brother's voice telling him he was happy where he was and that he didn't want his big brother worrying about him. It helped him tremendously then. The grief left his face and his shoulders became light after two thousand miles of tension.

On this drive to Virginia Beach, he called Karen in Phoenix from his cell phone. He truly believed that his sister knew everything and could find out anything she didn't know as fast as anyone alive, for Karen is an information hound. She would be his best advisor and could find his best leads on libraries that wanted him at book signings. Karen had told him that she would e-mail every public library in Virginia, even the ones that didn't carry his books, because she thought she could find her brother writing assignments from librarians who had money bequeathed to them from patrons. He told her he was wide open for anything and to see what she could find; and that he was even interested in that sidereal chart she was working on.

    Karen answered her phone at the Tempe branch:

    —Sister, Karen!

    —Dwayne! Where are you?

    —In Virginia Beach.

Karen listened to her brother tell her about Ann, Traveller, and brother John's voice telling him to go to Virginia Beach before the police found his stolen Winnebago. From her wheelchair Perry (a seat she'd had for two years, ever since her spinal cord dissolved), she listens while wearing a headset earplug.

    —That gives me the chills, Dwayne. I had a dream about Grandpa Dayne last night. I haven't dreamed about him since I was twelve.

    —That's a longshot, isn't it, Karen? Just because Grandpa's name was Edgar?

    —Isn't Cayce the one that said that dreams function to solve problems in waking life and to hasten the dreamer's new potentials?

    —You're on the Internet, right?

Karen laughed with her computer screen on an Edgar Cayce site.

    —Hey, ironsides, you got any library book signings for me?

    —Ironsides? Don't call me that. I don't like it.

    —I'm sorry.

    —You don't have many libraries in Virginia. The Fredericksburg Library is interested in a signing this Friday night.

    —Book it. Call me back and let me know what time.

    —Listen, Dwayne. I did your chart. I plugged in your time of birth in Woodbury and it matched with Fredericksburg in prosperity.

—What do you mean?

—It's the place most suitable for you to prosper now.

—What color is the line?

—Green.

—Like money.

—Yeah. That's the best place for your first book signing.

—What's the director's name?

—Addie Cousins, Karen said. She says your books rculate well there. I told her I'd fax a flyer to her about the gning for her to post in her library. Hold on bro..I have to check t a patron. He could hear his sister's wheelchair move on the exican tile, then, he heard her promoting his books to one of her trons:

—You ever read any of D. H. Dayne's novels?

o answer; she continued:

—Check his books out sometime. Dayne. D. H. He's my other.

hen she was finished scanning the patron's books, she rolled over her computer screen at her desk and picked up the phone:

—You say this girl's last name is Bruin...as in bear?

—Yeah...the cops verified her name from her social security mber.

—You say she worked at the Portland Public Library?

—In Oregon. Wait a minute. Come to think of it, she ght be from Portland, Maine. Try both.

—Does she have a middle name?

—I don't know.

—You slept with this woman and you don't know her me, Dwayne?

—I didn't sleep with her.

—Oh, you were going to boink her on the road.

—Karen, I don't feel like jokin's with you now.

—I'll get what I can on her and call ya later.

Bye, bro...love you.

—Love you, too.

—Oh, brother Dwayne! I have a library fact for ya. Write this down: Americans spend nine times as much on home video games ($1.5 billion) as they do on school library materials for their children.

After Dwayne finished scribbling down the fact:

—Bye, Karen.

—Dwayne?

—Yeah.

—Be careful.

She was known as Karen Bayer at work; but now, with her laptop on her insensate thighs, she was Karen Dayne, a protective sister scrambling to find all the information she could on this young wench who dared to rip off her brother. On a hunch: Karen found an Ann Bruin listed as a Tempe Library patron where her brother used to go when he lived with their brother John. Could she be the same girl? In my library? Karen wondered.

Within a minute, Karen had Ann's social security number from the Asheville Library records on employees. Soon, Karen had a list printed of all the books Ann Bruin checked out from the Tempe Library and in Asheville. Ann had checked out her brother's first two novels in Tempe, and his third book in Asheville. It wasn't that strange to check out a writer's books, but this was more than a coincidence, so, Perry Mason kept digging.

Forty-five minutes later, at the Virginia Beach Police station, he saw his parked silver Adventurer behind a fenced holding area. Her car was on the trailer; he looked and saw that she had North Carolina plates. He had the police drive her car off his trailer, then Dwayne drove Lawn Boy onto the trailer. An officer went inside Traveller with Dwayne to see if anything was

amaged or missing; all of his writing was in place. The officer left
wayne alone in Traveller after he signed a damage/loss report
rm, and told the writer that he could pick up his keys inside the
tation when he came in to press charges against Ms. Bruin.

He sat at his booth table in Traveller, where but two nights
go they drank wine and talked for hours. His mind was racing to
e Edgar Cayce retreat near the beach, near motel row; his
rother's excited voice telling him to go to Edgar in Virginia
each; and the brown eyes of Ann Bruin—the eyes he believed
ould love and adore him on his journey over North America.

Just then: his cell phone rang. Sister Karen's voice boomed
ith news. He listened, numb by the words coming from his sister
fter a dozen phone calls from her shotgun research. A nurse at
an Diego's Balboa Hospital was positive that Ann Bruin was the
ame abandoned baby Jane Doe that Dwayne had set up a trust
nd for from the book sales of his first novel. The nurse said that
nn had contacted her about the money left to her after finding an
d newspaper article on microfiche in a San Diego library. Karen
ld her brother to get away from that girl, that she was stalking
im for the money, and she could be dangerous.

Why go to all this trouble?, he wanted to ask her, and for
st a thousand bucks. Then it hit him: with the interest over
venty-one years, it could be a pretty big chunk of change. And
hat was more strange was her coming back into his life out of the
lue. It was just like his character Barney Cole, the federal systems
spector who returned. Barney blew into that Kansas hick town
nd rescued the protagonist Leonard, freeing him from his jail cell.
ad she read that book, too? He wondered.

When he reached the sergeant's front desk, his knees were
s weak as pudding:

—I don't want to press charges against Ms. Bruin.
he confused sergeant's eyes asked why.

—I just remembered I told her she could take it to Virginia

Beach to visit a friend. I had a few glasses of wine..and..I forgot.

—A friend? Funny how she never mentioned you gave her permission.

—Officer, I don't want to press charges. It's a big misunderstanding. Can you release her, please?

He paced around Traveller for nearly two hours before she came out of the station. She walked toward him twisting her canvas purse against her thigh, her gait slowing when she saw him leaning against her driver's-side door. Her apparent insouciant demeanor, he saw right through it, and called her on it when she stopped and stood some six feet away with her car keys in hand.

—You even care why I didn't press charges?
No answer. Her brown eyes looked down to the pavement as he talked to her softly with his arms folded in front of his chest.

—You ever read *White Shoulders*, my first novel?
A long pause of nothing. Then, she looked into his eyes and nodded yes.

—I never sold any to libraries. How'd you get a copy?
More nothing.

—And you're that baby girl who was abandoned in San Diego, the one I set up the trust fund for?
She nodded yes, her eyes low. He thought about that a few moments before he said:

—It was a thousand dollars. With interest, I don't know how much it would be today.

—About seven thousand, she said straight into his eyes.

—You took off with my motor home for seven thousand dollars? What made you think you could do that and get away with it?

—I planned to go with you awhile, take my car, and see if I could tell you who I was. I found out about the trust fund for me in an old newspaper article when I was nineteen. I believed I'd have the money when I was twenty-one, even though my parents who adopted me denied that I was the abandoned baby.

—How do you know you were?

—I know.

—Why go to all this trouble for seven grand?

—You were the closest connection to my birth parents.

—I didn't know your parents.

—I know. Your book–it was an escape for me. I knew that whoever my parents were, they had to be pretty much like the characters in that story.

He looked away from her while he thought about his next move and how he had this opportunity to make good on that money he knew that he really owed her. He surprised her:

—I'll make a deal with ya: You go with me for one week on the road an I'll give you the seven grand. No obligations or hassles. I want a week to explain what happened and to find out all about your life.

He extended his hand:

—Deal?

She thought about his character Josie's line in his novel *The Paper Man* and returned:

—Separate beds?

He picked up on it, smiling back:

—Separate beds, he agreed.

She accepted his handshake.

—You can follow me in your car, he said.

—I think I'm out of gas.

—Follow me to the station, he said.

A quick positive nod, then she watched him walk over to Traveller. He appeared true to his word, a connection true to his writing she felt she could trust. She told herself that she had no right not trusting him after he let her off the hook for stealing his RV.

After gassing up, she was still in his side-view mirror when they approached the Edgar Cayce Institute. The clean/white Cayce Hospital, built in 1928, now the headquarters for the Association for Research and Enlightenment and the Reilly School of Massotherapy. This was the place that maintains the psychic readings of the sleeping prophet, Edgar Cayce.

The gift shop for tourists and meditation gardens was off to the right; he parked Traveller at the base of a terraced slope in front of the Cayce Hospital, a splendid building that was as white as the scudding clouds behind it.

Now he so wanted to tell Ann about Karen's sidereal chart for finding him places to go; and that when he called his sister from his cell phone in the Virginia Beach Police station, she told him that his chart for family/past lives crossed Danville, Virginia. And to explain how Karen would use her computer to find the libraries where his books were circulating, then match the figures with his birth sign to determine if he should go there. These were areas she tracked with different colors shooting out in all directions on a computerized map of North America, emanating from his place of birth in Western Iowa; it looked like a fountain of colorful airline flight patterns.

Each color represents something different: Blue represents spirit, the blue line crossing the best areas Dwayne should be in order to enhance spirit, a line that originated from his birthplace and represents spirit relationship to God the Creator; green represents prosperity, his best places to prosper; health is gold, the reason Dwayne moved to Asheville; pink is passion/career; brown is home the best place to settle; black is mind, the best cerebral place; purple is mystery, his favorite color on the chart because of his propensity to write mysteries; yellow is family/past lives. And from the chart Karen faxed him: a yellow line ran from Iowa in two directions, on direction shot north into North Dakota and Canada and the other went east through Virginia.

After parking in the Cayce parking lot, he caught himself thinking about Johnny again, and how his brother once remarked how they could live together in their old age since they probably would never marry.

He took a copy of Karen's chart from his visor and glanced to his side-view mirror and saw Ann appearing tense behind the wheel of her Escort, her hands clenched tight at the top of her steering wheel as she parked next to Traveller.

He looked down at San Diego on his chart, where Ann was abandoned; he saw a purple line running through it.

—Mystery, he whispered. She is that, he muttered with a wry smile on his face.

He hopped out of Traveller and began to walk with her toward the Cayce meditation gardens behind the gift shop, forgetting for the moment that this is the place that his brother's voice told him to go.

—We can park here for the night, he told her. Do ya wanna go for a walk on the beach?

She smiled and went back to her car to get a pullover sweater. As Dwayne's eyes went to the meditation gardens, a sudden dawning was coming to him and lost before he could realize it as he walked over to her car. He could see that she had piled her clothes on the back seat of her car. Other things were jammed in the car as if she had packed in a big hurry. She could leave her clothes there, he thought, not wanting to clutter his beautiful new home with her belongings.

After crossing the busy road in front of the institute, it was only a hundred yards to the beach. They walked barefoot on the wet sand; he had removed his shoes after she did. The heavy sand was cold, invigorating, just when the October sun was nearly down and the ocean breeze cool and constant. He asked her if she'd heard of Cayce's work.

—Yes, a little. I know he'd go into a trance and prescribe

-103-

treatment for all kinds of ailments. He was some kind of psychic healer.

—I first began paying attention to my dreams more after reading about his miracles. About a year before my brother died I would have dreams about the letters WY. I didn't know if it stood for Wyoming or why or even what why was about. This WY would come and go a few times in dreams..and I'd catch myself thinking about what it meant. I'd usually be startled by it when it came up. It felt like some kind of warning to some really bad thing coming. I really thought it had something to do with Wyoming, that maybe I'd move there. In *Missouri Madness* I used the WY, I thought cleverly, in my storyline. It was right at the time I was proofing my final draft of the book that my brother committed suicide.

—I'm so sorry.

—I know, because I was worried about him the weeks before and worried about my mother worrying about him. That's why I lost the hold I had on *Missouri Madness*. That's when he was losing his will to live. I let the story lose its plausibility, foisting it off onto the pages. All because my brother thought he was a cowboy...like John Wayne, a man alone against the world. The WY did represent Wyoming, the cowboy. I know this now. My dreams were about his impending death. Most things can be corrected. Not this. So, I pay attention now. Anyway, I knew the WY was not for my story. It was for my life. I ignored the warning about his death. Then, his voice told me to go to Cayce's. Not much later, the cops told me they had you and my motor home in Virginia Beach. Maybe that's why I want to believe in my sister's chart. To get some kind of order to this madness. I really feel her chart can get me back to my brother somehow..and make my life meaningful here...somehow understand it all.

—Maybe it was telling you to come here, Ann smiled.

He turned to her as they walked under the chalky gray dusk, above the wet rush of this blue merle ocean tide that chilled their bare ankles.

—Did you know you were coming here? he asked.

—Sort of.

—What do you mean, sort of?

She looked into his pale blue eyes that were so tired from worry and confusion and said:

—I heard the same voice.

—My brother's voice?

—I don't know.

—What was it like..the voice? Was it a male voice?

—Yeah, kinda high pitched, excited like. Like a little boy.

—That's him! When did he tell you to come here?

—While I was putting my stuff in my car, when I last left my apartment.

—What, exactly, did he say?

—Go to Virginia Beach. See Edgar Cayce.

—Why didn't you say something at the gas station when I said I wanted to stop at the Cayce Institute?

—I don't know. I thought it was a coincidence.

—My brother told me to come here to see Edgar.

He stopped and took her hand and turned her around to see the bright white buildings of the Cayce Institute in the distance. He told her how, about a year ago, he asked his sister to find a place on her chart for him, a place where he could heal and enhance his writing.

—That chart told me I should be in Asheville, he said. This voice you heard..whether or not it's my brother..could be all about making good on the money I owe you and clearing my past so I can move on and really prosper. I truly believe that, Ann. My brother's death has something to do with my prosperity.

He let go of her hand when he felt her lack of warmth and desire to his touch. He knew she did not trust him, and that was understand-able; and, he picked up on her aversion to their age disparity.

   When their cold feet reached the boardwalk, a wide sidewalk of clean cement, some sixty yards from the bay, she hurried over and into a hotel lobby to use the restroom. He waited on a bench on the boardwalk, thinking about writing a scene about his brother, the first memory he had of his brother. He took a look at his memory while his eyes stayed on the sand sticking between his toes, the roar of the surf whooshing beneath his memory. He felt himself spinning a bit, counterclockwise, back, and back, compelled to really see this memory and write it down later:

   It was springtime in the early 60s. Dwayne was eight or nine, about the age of Ben in *Ledges*. It was on the same farm as Dutch's farm in *Ledges* in the central farmyard area. Ten-month-old Johnny was sitting in his stroller, his big, bald head so round, and turned to his big brother Dwayne who was kicking a fat, worn football high into the air. This ball was bloated, in places: black rubber bubbles protruded out of the cover in two or three places. Baby Johnny was so happy just watching the kick and then the ball sailing so high. This one particular kick was in slow motion and headed right for that massive head of brother Johnny. Dwayne watched in horror as the ball knocked his brother backwards in his stroller, chipping out the bottom corner of a new front tooth. Dwayne ran over to his crying brother and wiped his bloody lip with his trembling hand as Johnny screamed from pain and fear even after being picked up; all because he was so mad at his big brother for making this terrible thing come his way and turn his world upside down.

   —He was mad at me, Dwayne mumbled while coming out of his reverie just as Ann was walking toward him.
She looked happier, as if the mention of Edgar had eliminated her

-106-

listress from being in jail, or something like that.

—There used to be a health food store around the corner, ae pointed. Let's see if it's still there and get some good food. You must be hungry.

—I am.

In the store they each carried a basket. He told her to get what she wanted. She liked tofu and she told him she'd make them a tofu salad.

Each carried a bag filled mostly with vegetables. On their walk back to Traveller, he asked her if she ever found out who abandoned her. She nodded no, not saying anything, until a few steps more:

—I figure it must've been my mother who abandoned me. I aever have had a desire to find her. I look at it as if I was lucky.

—How's that?

—I was adopted by a good couple. I considered them my parents in every way. I've never lost anyone close to me. Not big osses. Never had a really serious boyfriend..so no bad breakups. I lon't get too close to people.

—You don't get hurt that way. You're still young. You eem so sweet. But takin' off to find me and stealin' Traveller.. hat took some guts. I still don't get it. Why all that for a few housand bucks, Ann?

He could see that she was choosing her words carefully. They walked a ways before she gave him two reasons:

—You were the closest thing to my birth parents. I thought ou kept the money for me in a San Diego bank, and I thought my eal parents, or one of them, got in touch with you when they saw he news article about my trust fund. When I found out the bank vas out of business, I got mad. I kept thinking of your book when 3arney found Leonard in that small Kansas town. And I thought 'd find you and get my money and see what you were like. For me, a few thousand dollars is a lot of money. I can go to school or start somewhere new with a little security.

—Nothin' personal, but how do I know you are the same baby girl who was abandoned?

—Does it matter?

—Yeah, it matters, if yer scammin' me.

—How many books did you sell by telling your readers you were raising money for me?

—Yeah, I'll give ya that. But I don't trust anybody after what my brother did. And anybody includes me. After I put that grand in the bank in a trust fund for you, let's say it's you, I kept selling my books, telling prospects I was giving part of the money to child abuse prevention. I used that cause to sell books. That's why I want to find out about your life. And if your life had child abuse in it—like I think it did—then giving you the money still clears my debt, even if you're not the same girl.

—What makes you think I was treated bad?

—Oh, I don't know. Maybe stealin' my RV for starters.

They said nothing for a block, yet a quarter mile from Traveller. Dwayne was waiting for her to say something. She finally did:

—If I can prove that I'm the one you sold books for, will you give me the money tomorrow?

—Yeah.

Dwayne spotted the same acacia tree atop a hill a hundred yards from the Cayce parking lot on the Cayce property. Years ago, when Dwayne came here, he was told how Edgar would sit and lean against its trunk because of its healing energy. He pointed:

—I want to sit by that tree for a bit.

They sat together, their backs against the slim trunk. Not far from the base of the old tree stood a lone bunch of drooping purple Delphiniums, their kelly green stems two feet tall, slowly moving in the bay breeze on green stilts that were recently planted y some Cayce employee who recently lost a loved one.

She started to talk about her proof about being the
bandoned baby; he could see and feel her words:

It was the early 1980s. Dwayne was selling his first novel
oor-to-door in one of those endless subdivisions in Orange
County. He was having a good day, though hot–so were sales. He
nocked on the front door of this particular house, feeling an eye
n him from the peephole; since in a cul de sac he surprised a lot of
rospects, so he had to look harmless. This particular prospect she
vas talking about, he could remember him: a man in his early 30s,
vho, after reading the writer's laminated news article about the
bandoned baby and his pledge to give a grand to her trust fund, he
alled his wife to the door. After she read the article, the couple
mbraced and began crying in their front doorway. The man
rought Dwayne a glass of water and they bought all of the five
ooks he had left in his sales case.

(Dwayne really knew for certain that Ann was the
bandoned girl when she told him that the generous couple are her
doptive parents and that she was taking a nap in her crib at the
ime he was there.)

He remembered finding a little tree like this acacia, in a
lace to sit in the shade and cry after that emotional sale. The
tress from his door-to-door campaign had been pent up and
eleased by that loving couple. And he knew that nobody else
ould know that, and even at the time, the couple never said that
hey had adopted the abandoned girl. Ann told Dwayne her
doptive parents told her that story when she graduated from high
chool. That's when they decided that she was old enough to know
bout her abandonment.

Then the clincher: When they reached Traveller she got a
opy of his first book *White Shoulders* from her car trunk; she told
im her parents gave it to her when she graduated. Inside the front

cover, Dwayne recognized his dated signature and his familiar words: "Thanks for your help," and, the book was signed to "Ann." He remembered that sale in particular, because it was his biggest residential sale ever; rarely did he ever sell more than one book to a resident. And he recalled signing the books to different people for that couple.

Later: as she made the tofu salad in Traveller at the counter by the sink, Dwayne sat aloof at the booth table behind her; her copy of *White Shoulders* was on the table in front of him. As he began to write out Ann's check for seven thousand dollars, she could hear him crying, holding back until he wrote *White Shoulders* on the check's memo line. She went over to him. He handed her the check. She sat next to him and held him as he sobbed uncontrollably, blubbering out his words:
—Thank you, Ann. Thank you. I'm so glad you found me. Thank you.

After their meal, they went out to the Cayce meditation gardens. They sat directly across from each other on wooden benches. The space between them was perhaps ten feet. They were surrounded by Daylilies: reds and pinks of Almond Buff, Always Afternoon, and Amber Love; and the whites and yellows of Ardent Affair; the deep reds of Bess Ross and Big Apple; along with the violet of Beyond the Blue.
Ann closed her eyes; he then closed his. Her mind was reciting a positive affirmation that closes off negative influences and allows divine influences into the auric field. To herself:
—I am in control. I am the only authority in my life. I am divinely protected by the light of by Being. I close off my aura and body of light to all but my own God self. Thank you, God.

Dwayne's mind was back to that house, her house, in

Orange County. His imagination was at work; for D. H.
Dayne—his meditation:

Back to that day he sold her parents five books. He was
invited inside by the nice couple who adopted Ann. He sat down
on the white sofa in a white-tiled living room filled with crystals and
framed pen and ink originals of unicorns. The couple had gone into
their bedroom and had closed the door behind them.. quietly.
Soon, from behind their closed bedroom door, a familiar song
began to play until it played on the living room stereo speakers.
The song had a baby crying at the very beginning of the song. It
was Steve Wonder's song *Isn't She Lovely*, the same song he used
in his book *White Shoulders*.

He sat in the couple's house, alone, listening to that song
with an ever-widening smile, ending his scene there.

As he breathed deeply in the meditation gardens, his
thoughts were racing, mainly because of where he was: in the
garden of "The Sleeping Prophet," Edgar Cayce. I know I'm not
psychic, Dwayne told himself; however, he had to pay attention
now. His mind had just shown him that scene. How could that
couple who adopted Ann know that song was in my book? He
reminded himself that it's not real. But then: he remembered in that
book *White Shoulders*, that the song played during a commercial to
raise money for the prevention of child abuse after a little girl in San
Francisco was killed by her abusive father. He wondered if this
could mean that Ann was abused. There was no time to find out.
She had proven to him that she was the girl he pledged to raise
money for.

—The debt is paid, he whispered, dismissing the notion that
she was lying about who she was.

When a jet flew overhead he opened his eyes just enough to
see her sitting there with the back of her brown hands on her lap,
her fingers relaxed and curled as if she held a delicate flower in

them. D. H. Dayne's memory trapped her in this gentle repose; he made a mental note to write about what he saw. Had she really heard his brother's voice, too? he wondered, as the incredible nape of her brown neck held his focus.

He closed his eyes and thought about how Ann was meditating like his character Josie did in *The Paper Man*. And he thought of how he is not meditating, not quieting his mind at all; but rather, filling his mind with visual images to always remember —when she's gone tomorrow.

Then, as Dwayne focused on his breath more and more, Ann was visualizing each color of her seven chakras while taking twenty-three breaths for each color and for each year of her life. She had been doing this since she was nineteen, a year after she found out she was adopted. Meanwhile:

In her Phoenix apartment, Karen was all the way back in her recliner. Karen could walk, barely; she had to be in a wheelchair at work, so she left Perry there by the employee entrance to the library. Now, she was stroking the back of her orange and white cat Florence while staring blankly at a movie. She was thinking hard about her brother and that girl Ann Bruin. Something to Karen still didn't click. Karen was psychic, more so at night in her dreams. Her constant pain in her neck and lower back, with numbness in her fingers, flared when she was awake. Always. Her best medication: prayer. Her incessant prayers kept her from being a "tuna," she called it.

As she made her way into her bedroom in pain, she smirked at the nickname Ironsides that her brother gave her. And he also gave her Perry Mason because of her investigative skills and her penchant for being defensive.

With Florence purring on her pillow, her legs elevated, Ironsides went to sleep praying for her brother, the brother who had already immortalized her in his novel *Ledges* as sister Pam. In

Ledges, eight-year-old Pam had traits Karen at first wished her brother had left out of his popular book: She has a club foot and limps; she's overweight; she flatulated often to annoy her brother; she was a daddy's girl, dependent on her father's attention; devious and manipulative; she was sexually abused by a wicked blind man; and—they were all true.

What angered Karen the most: Ben, her older brother in *Ledges*, was this sensitive and caring protector of their little family. That was sometimes true, but that wasn't the whole story. Dwayne had been an abusive brother in many ways. Karen overlooked it today, all of it: the fighting, teasing and cruel insults over an eight-year period when their mother was raising them alone on little money.

Before falling off to sleep, Karen remembered the time fourteen-year-old Dwayne gave her a bloody nose when he punched her for refusing to help do the dishes in their mobile home. She was mad and surprised him when he dared her to hit him. She did. It still made her laugh to think about it as she now fell off to sleep to the rhythm of Florence purring and the prayer for God to protect her brother.

In the Cayce parking lot, as Ann slept in the back bedroom with the door closed, Dwayne was at the booth writing a chapter in his next book. It was during his most difficult years. The chapter was titled "The Trailer." And he knew that the girl sleeping here was responsible for this creative mood he's in. He felt this way most times he was around her. Yes, Ann Bruin was responsible for his chapter he was able to see now. He knew where his pencil was leading him, and it was going to hurt.

The Trailer

—Yeah, the Fergusons have a new home. Big deal.

This was the typical cynical self-talk David Ferguson had created by sixteen.

This time of year, early November, was as dark as a prairie shithouse after basketball practice at Woodbury High. His hair, short for 1968, was still wet from his only shower today. He was chewing fast the candy bar he had just stolen from Koger's Drugstore, like some wet two-legged river rat, after buying a mint for two cents. Two or three times a week he would shoplift a treat for himself, and hardly would he feel any remorse. That's because he had trained himself to shut down most of his feelings, good and bad. Stealing was dangerous, and it paid off, for food at home would be scarce.

The Ferguson's new home was seventy feet long and called a double-wide. It looked better on the outside. They had been living in a one-bedroom cracker box stucco house for four months, off the main road a quarter mile in Stephensville, South Dakota, the roughest part of metro Woodbury located across the Little Sioux River under this bridge that was only a few degrees from freezing.

It was here, whenever he crossed the short bridge into South Dakota, he would think of the life they lived on Elmwood for two years; it was a very nice neighborhood in Woodbury. And he would dwell on how his life changed from bad to good, to bad, then good again, and now: very bad.

—Does life get worse the older you get?, he asked himself when he stepped into South Dakota.

He walked faster on the graveled dirt shoulder, passing four dive bars and a giant liquor store—all within a block of the bridge.

Yes, this was early November, not too cold, yet warm enough to let David's mind think of things other than the weather. Before he reached the turn under the black train trestle, he side-glanced back, across the road to the little trailer park where one of his best friends lived, Mike Steppe, a half-blood Indian-Italian who lived with his Italian mother and four sisters in a sardine trailer not half the size of his new double-wide. He thought of how crowded they must be in that place, sharing that little bathroom, and yet, there was always laughter, healthy fighting and arguments, and love. Love was definitely there. Mike's mother had made real love come alive in that dinky trailer.

As he turned his eyes back to his path, they raked past the tiny barber shop where he got his hair cut by that old barber who whistled and wheezed on his neck. And down a few doors from the barber shop was the town jail where Karl the part-time cop kept his white patrol car parked. Under the train trestle he thought of how his mother told him that this is the jailhouse where Donny, Aunt Cleone's son, hung himself when he was a cop there. He did it because he was jilted by his girlfriend. So creepy a subject that it was hardly ever mentioned.

David hit the dirt/gravel back road off the highway he always took. For a half mile he passes these little houses and trailers of the working class—families who mostly worked for the packing houses in the city. It's now that he hears Toby the friendly black shepherd barking at that black/brown mongrel stray, a collarless mutt that would attack the garbage cans out of reach of Toby's chain at the front of Toby's trailer. He couldn't see either dog as he walked, but he new the scene.

A couple months ago David had lured the stray mongrel in the back storage room of their stucco house. David kicked the dog several times for stealing Toby's rib bones when Toby's chain was wound around his dog house.

Now: David's neck was hot for punishing that starved dog,

for being cruel to the lean animal. He had not been cruel to a dog before, but this efferent thing came over him that choked away compassion from his heart. He had kicked that vagrant dog until it whined and crawled out the back door. He had no compassion; he was lost in anger and fear, so he would attack weak things like his brother and sister. He was sorry for all that, and sorry for the other cruel thing he had done last night. Pete would be okay, he hoped.

As the road got darker he came to the end of it and turned left onto the dirt lane hardened with winter tire ruts. There was his new home, on cement blocks, white with a charcoal black trim. All the lights were on. It was the second trailer from the end of a row of some two dozen trailers. Hull's semi was idling, as usual, parked beside their end trailer.

Since their mother worked nights tending bar in Nebraska, David ran the house. When he turned the loose chrome knob of the back door it was locked. He knocked softly and barked:

—Open the door!

He felt tired from his walk, beating himself up. When Karen opened the door:

—There better be some food left.

Karen lumbered her heavy frame back to her bedroom, staying away from her grouchy brother.

—How's Pete? he shouted back to his sister.

—What do you care? she returned.

He went down the narrow hallway to the kitchen and saw the blue parakeet Pete apparently recovered from his near heart attack, for last night: David, Karen and Johnny were watching Alfred Hitchcock's movie *The Birds* on their color TV in the living room. When the birds attacked the town, David impishly put Pete cage by the TV and turned up the volume, causing the little bird to flutter in a frenzy, sending blue feathers everywhere. Karen made big fuss, but David and little Johnny laughed at the sight. After David put Pete's cage back on its stand, all three kids watched the bird with spooked eyes as Pete tried to recover from Hitch's scene.

Now, Karen joined Johnny on the brown rayon sofa that folded into a day bed with this big crack at the fold that made it very uncomfortable. It was like trying to balance your weight on two uneven ironing boards if you slept there. David would put his little brother on it after he peed their bed in David and Johnny's bedroom; that usually happened every morning in the winter.

—I'm hungry, Dave, Johnny whined in that high pitch.

—So am I, runt. Make yerself somethin'.

—There's nothin'! Johnny whined louder.

—Tell Mom. Don't bother me about it.

From the living room they listened to their big brother open the refrigerator door. They couldn't see their brother's eyes disappointed and tired when he saw the Velveeta Cheese foil covering half of the remaining cheese with visible streaks of mayonnaise in several places. The near-empty mayonnaise jar stood beside a jar of pickle juice. There were a few hamburger buns, some butter sticks, a bowl of cooked white rice covered with foil, and a little milk. He opened the freezer. It held empty ice trays and mounds of frost. He slammed the empty cupboards. There was one other place to look.

Their mother's purses were numerous. She liked nice things. She had a closet full of nice clothes. David went through a dozen purses, looking for loose change. He found three bucks, enough to get three loosemeats and sodas at the roadside café.

Within a few minutes his brother and sister tramped behind him. They couldn't care less if their trailer was the nicest and newest on the lot. There were no street light, only hunger and the porch lights of the mismatched trailers along the way to the café. To their right: a twin-engine plane landed at the puddle-jumper airport behind them, its lights shining brightly in the Dakota moonlight.

At this moment, David was tense and didn't know he was.

His fear level was up whenever he left their world and escorted his clan into the world of strangers. His siblings never picked up on this fear. They thought their big brother was brave and strong and could protect them from harm. This false sense of security he gave them only helped protect them from feeling this intense fear that overcame brother David at times, until he learned to not fear. That's why he could kick a helpless dog until it crawled outside on its belly; that's how he could put Pete in Hitchcock's movie; and that's how he could show anger to those two mongrel brats left in his charge. If emotion is the place where the mind and body meet—then David Ferguson was 130 pounds of fear mixed with blood, water, bones, and shit.

Even when they entered the dark and greasy café, with not a vitamin or mineral under its roof, David had that despotic scowl fixed on his emotionless countenance, a look his siblings feared and the public ignored. Only Karen could loosen his face to a smile and a bright blush, which was a look so foreign and alarming to his family, they'd welcome back his angry scowl.

Johnny was the baby, and David was tough on him. He learned not to be a baby around David. Johnny's father was not Karen and David's father. Johnny was never considered a half-brother by Karen or David. Johnny's father was a prosperous hard working farmer, whose farm north of Onawa was situated on 600 of the best acres of land around. They lived on the farm for three years. When Johnny was two, their mother left the farm with her three kids and received separate maintenance from Johnny's father. So, at the front of the month the food was plenty; but this was the end of the early part of the month. So, here they sit on counter stools at the roadside café, the only customers, eating their loosemeats and drinking orange pop, with their mother's loose change found in her closet in the newest double-wide in Stephensville.

He remembered he left his chapter "The Trailer" on
raveller's table. He remained quiet on the leather sofa, stretching
s legs as he saw Ann making coffee. He got out of bed in his
oxers, pulling on his jeans and shirt, noticing his pages were still in
ie same place on top of the table.

—Good morning! she smiled.

—How'd you sleep? he asked.

—Great! Better than last night, she smiled, referring to jail.

She made them breakfast: coffee with toast and tofu that
iey shared at the table booth.

—I did sleep really well last night...for the first time in a
ing time. I think it's because you gave me that money so
asily...after stealing Traveller...and not pressing charges.

—Duh...ya think so? he laughed. Resolving that part of my
ast has given me some peace. Thank you, he smiled.
he put her hand out on the table; he put his hand on hers and held
. They smiled into the eyes of new friends and he said:

—Since my brother died I pay more attention to my
ioughts and feelings. And my dreams sometimes tell me things.
ast night it came to me before I went to sleep...after I wrote that
ie pointed to his pages). I had this aunt, Aunt Cleone, who told
iy mother we were related to Robert E. Lee. She told her just
efore she died about ten years ago. When I was in my roaring
0s...I came here to Cayce's to learn more about past lives. I found
iyself prowling the battlefields where Lee fought: Cold Harbor,
he Wilderness...even Gettysburg. And I went to Lee's birthplace
tratford on his birthday. I wanted to know all about his life. I
ven named this RV after his favorite horse—Traveller. The more I

learned about him, the more I knew I had this connection to him, even though I was born in the north. My brother and I played over a thousand games of backgammon where he was Grant and I was Lee.

—Who won? she asked, her eyes interested in his story.

—Oh, Grant did...in the long run. But I won some important battles. Anyway, my brother truly was Unconditional Surrender Grant; he would never give up in a backgammon game, no matter how bad he was getting beat. I would...if hopeless. My brother wouldn't...he'd never surrender. And yet, my brother surrendered his life. And my point is: three times in my life I was driving near Appomattox where Lee surrendered to Grant, but could never quite go there. Something was telling me "Not now, later, when you have someone with you to share it with." I don't know if this is something I should do now to forgive my brother... or forgive myself, or because of some past life pain related to General Lee.

Ann stated mater-of-factly:

—It could be where you surrender your past.

She watched him thinking about his next words:

—If you could...I'm ready to go to Appomattox and see. I'll pay for your gas. It's not that far from here. I could go with you to the bank to help cash your check...and then you could follow me there.

She thought about her words carefully, then spoke softer, leaning toward him across the table top:

—Whatever happened then and whatever happens in the future was and will be in the present. I do believe in past lives and living in the present.

—So do I, Ann. I know that time is manmade, unreal... because we only have right now. That's why I'm asking you right now to go to Appomattox...and see what happens now.

Dwayne told her that after he wrote the chapter "The

Trailer," he felt that something was pulling at him, to write about things only imagined or that possibly came from a past life. When he asked him if he believed in reincarnation, he said:

—After my brother died I stopped believing in anything that required faith, because to believe is to have faith without proof. He went on to say that these spots, these places his sister Karen found on her chart...somehow charged him with this desire to get down on paper whatever he saw, or he would be spun dizzily to the ground and be forced to see things his subconscious demanded he see right now. He said he really noticed it last night when he went to bed. As he wrote "The Trailer" this spinning appeared like it would begin if he even thought about stopping the flow of his writing. He told her about a passage he had read long ago, something the writer Zane Grey wrote about places: that places had sustained life, and were, perhaps, just as important as the people who had lived in these places. And he told Ann that our past is a past life, to learn from, but to not let it diminish our lives in the present. And he told her how he promised himself that he would never tell a soul about these mental cyclones, these tornadoes in his mind that would spin him into these dizzying whirlwinds of places related to things he had or should have written about. He said that he saw these scenes while in this cyclone, as if they were camera shots to be filmed from a script, but were lacking the depth of characters and narrative a novel demands.

Then, something she asked him:

—How was your vision when in these cyclones?

—That's strange, because things were not so clear in his reality back then. My vision was really bad. Often I didn't wear my glasses because I didn't want to see some things. Like my character David in "The Trailer" was not wearing his glasses...but he could see clearly.

Dwayne asked her if she'd read what he wrote last night. She did. And she agreed that what he had written he had truly

-121-

seen. But it was as if he was writing about what he only wanted to see, not at all covering the whole reality of what was there.

Ann twisted open the blinds and looked outside at the Cayce parking lot. She told him that after she cashed her check she'd go with him to Appomattox, but after that, she'd hit the road

She followed Traveller to Blackstone, Virginia, a few miles off Highway 460 just 50 miles from Appomattox. They sat across from each other at a booth in a café that Dwayne had lunch in the last time he was near Lee and Grant's famous meeting place.

He told her that ever since he found out that she was the abandoned girl he lost his attraction to be with her. Now, he was really glad she was not going along with him on the road, and, after cashing her check at a Blackstone bank before coming to this table, he wished he hadn't asked her to go along to Appomattox.

At their table, she told him how she went to Phoenix for a week to look him up and that she planned to confront him about her trust fund. Instead, she lost her nerve and checked out two of his books at the Tempe Library, reading them in two days.

She could see and feel that he was anxious about something and called him on it:

—You seemed occupied. What's up?

—I don't know. Last time I was here I felt this way. That's why I didn't go to Appomattox.

Dwayne put a twenty-dollar bill on the table to cover their tab, then said that he had to go to the Blackstone Library to see how his books are circulating and to place his new book there.

She watched him leave the café; she could see him get a copy of his new book from the trunk of Lawn Boy. Something felt bad to her. She waited for him.

Meanwhile: Karen was at work in Perry her wheelchair, pounding away on her laptop keyboard. She had finished Ann Bruin's astral sidereal chart and was switching back and forth from er brother's chart to Ann's chart, comparing where their lines intersected after enlarging Virginia on her screen. She could see that they had lines in common in several places. Karen would switch back to Ann's place of birth or abandonment in San Diego. Since Karen couldn't be sure of Ann's exact time of birth, she could only use the day that Ann was found in San Diego. Then: she saw Dwayne's purple/mystery line crossing paths with Ann's purple/mystery line in San Diego. To herself:

—Two intersecting purples equals a black...trouble in the mind.

She knew that this meant that her brother was going to have his mind blown in Virginia...somewhere. Quickly: Karen dialed her brother's cell phone, but she could not get through. She started to pray as:

D. H. Dayne was walking down Blackstone's Main Street, like ten thousand other Main Streets in his America.. He still felt his anxiousness and dread that comes from certain doom. He used to feel this way when he first became a salesman and the last time he was in Blackstone. And he had it when his phone rang in Asheville, giving him the shock of his life, when he first heard of his brother's suicide.

Just two days before, when Johnny lay on his couch rotting for two days with a bullet in his brain, two days before their mother would find him, Dwayne muttered to himself:

—He's better off dead.

Now, in this fractious state, Dwayne got quick directions to the library from a local passing by on the sidewalk.

The three blocks to the Blackstone Library were lined with thirty-foot dogwoods, their slender trunks wrapped in bark resembling alligator hide, rough with deep grooves.

Just then: facts and images he never knew as Dwayne Dayne were coming into his consciousness. He was now so paranoid of these things; he tried to block them out. For starters, he believed Ann had put something in his coffee at the café. His breathing became labored, and his brow became hot and perspiring. From another time or life he knew that the dogwood when soaked in whiskey was used to relieve attacks of malaria. He walked over to one of the dogwoods that appeared the most fulgent and embraced the lean trunk, wrapping his body around its waffled bark after letting his invoice pad and new book drop to the ground.

He kept his hot forehead pressed against the dogwood, his eyes fluttering until he closed them tightly. The brain of D. H. Dayne was now as the dogwood leaf when gently broken, its silky threads pulling out from the veins.

So clearly: he could see Johnny's face, the face of a proud brother who taught him his harshest lesson in this life: to make peace with those you love, because they may die and leave you alone in the light and darkness, creep into your mind at work and play, reminding the brother left behind that he was somehow part of the reason he left you...forever.

Emotions shifted fast, to his eyes. Oh, why couldn't this gush from my mouth and be done with in a few hurling heaves, and soak forever into the earth and be gone, away from me, he cried inwardly. Why does it have to redden my face and drip from my eyes, the eyes I never saw him with, he wailed to himself. Then:

—I wouldn't see you, Johnny! he bawled, his scarred eyes closed with streams of liquid toxins running down his cheeks while hugging the sturdy dogwood with all his strength in his quaking arms.

It seemed like hours had passed when he entered the Blackstone Library. He did not care if he was detaining Ann, in fact, if she was gone when he returned—so be it. This time he had Traveller's keys in his pocket. He greeted the lady behind the counter as if she could be the librarian or director:

—Hi! Are you the librarian or director?

—Yes, she smiled. May I help you?

He was taking on the personality of his character Floyd in his novel *The Paper Man* when he smiled:

—I sure hope so. I'm D. H. Dayne from Asheville.

He paused to see if she recognized his name. She didn't.

—You bought my first three titles from me when I called you.

—Oh, yes.

—I have a new book that just came out.

She went to her screen to check circulation on his books. Circs were good. He left his new book with her and told her that Karen his sister handled his accounts now and that the address in Phoenix was now his new mailing address to send her check to the address in his invoice.

He left the library after telling her he was headed to a book signing in Fredericksburg.

When he returned to the café, Ann was reading the copy of his new book that he gave her earlier.

—You like it so far? he asked.

—Yes, I want to read more.

—Good. But I guess we better be goin'.

—To Appomattox? she asked.

He nodded yes. She noticed that he looked different somehow.

—Somethin's different about you.

—I sold my new book to the library.

He wanted to talk about his ordeal on the way to the library, but he didn't.

—So...you'll follow me? he said.

—Let's go, she smiled.

On highway 460, behind the wheel of Traveller and closing in on Appomattox, Dwayne tried to call Karen, but he couldn't get through.

Ann was in his side-view mirror following at a safe distance. He noticed that his body was unusually tired; particularly, his legs ached as if he'd been running. Soon, his breathing became labored. He considered pulling over and telling Ann he needed to rest, but he kept on.

After passing a highway marker that read Appomattox 6 miles, he stroked his chin and felt a full beard had grown on his face. He flipped down his mirror on his visor and saw that his face had aged considerably with this gray/white beard; his hair was nearly all white. Then, he nearly drove off the shoulder into the ditch when he saw that his eyes were now brown, a liquid butterscotch color; they were the eyes of a terrible sadness, of surrender after so many sacrifices. He knew them. They were Marse Robert's eyes, Robert E. Lee.

He tried Karen again. His cell phone was dead. Before he turned into the entrance to Appomattox, he looked into his side-view mirror and could not see Ann's car. The paved parking area for Appomattox became covered in lime-colored fog. Zero visibility and a throbbing headache forced him to park before he hit something.

When he opened Traveller's door to get out, his legs gave out under him, sending him sprawling to the hard ground that was now cold dirt that smelled of horseshit and gunpowder. The earth began to spin under him, faster and faster until he became nauseous. He closed his eyes and could not scream for it to stop. Then, just before he passed out: he thought of Ann and how she must've spiked his food or coffee.

For this was no dream, and this was not his imagination. He could hear the rattle of artillery miles away to the south. When he heard the word "surgeon" he opened his eyes and could now see the dusty butternut uniforms of these lean Confederate officers. He wanted to say:

—My great great grandpa is General Lee. I'm not him. For ᵉ knew nothing of the battles behind him or the strategy ahead. D. . Dayne was here to complete something, and he was not ɔnscious of what that something is. He kept his mouth shut and ₃tened while the officers helped him onto an unfinished cedar ɔotstool. He was not going to initiate anything, for he knew he ᵃas Dwayne Dayne incarnate and that he'd been somehow ᵃnsported back in time to Appomattox.

At that instant: a rebel courier on horseback came galloping ᵥer to them:

—Sir, General Grant will be here soon to discuss terms of ₃rrender.

ᵂayne could see the faces of the men around him; they looked isconsolate and ashamed of the word "surrender." Each man's ᵧes were on the ground, averted from who they thought was their ₑloved leader.

How can he possibly pretend to be "The Gray Fox?"

—Where's Traveller? Dwayne asked in a natural soft ᵛirginia drawl.

—Having breakfast, sir, one of his staff answered.

—I'll take a ride. Bring him to me, Dwayne said softly.

In the distance he could see the white McClean farmhouse ₑing readied for this historical meeting, perhaps the most ₙportant meeting in American warfare. Some Confederate officers ᵥere primping and polishing and beating the dust off each other on ₑe McClean front porch.

Then: Dwayne stood when he saw the loyal gray charger of ᴹarse Robert being led by his bridle toward him. Traveller was ₐller and wider than he imagined, and his eyes were blue/black and ₙtelligent. So intelligent: the horse shuddered and snorted from ᵂayne's touch. None of the rebels noticed that this man is two ₙches taller than their commander.

Dwayne's legs were weak when he took to the saddle,

mounting Traveller while saying:

—I'll return forthright.

The men saluted him. He did not return their salute; he was too absorbed in just how in the hell he'd gotten there and "forthright"... I've never said forthright in my life, he told himself.

Traveller stayed at a slow walk, taking him down a row of scraggly crab apple trees, stopping for his rider to pick one of the green apples. After feeding one to Traveller he put one in his coat pocket. He removed a daguerreotype photo he found inside the pocket. As Traveller moved on, Dwayne studied the photo of the young girl, her brown curls touching her forehead, and that sweet look of innocense so apparent in her eyes.

—Annie, Dwayne mumbled.

He knew Annie was Lee's young daughter who died during the war, though he had never seen a photo of her that he could recall. Consciously he had no memories of Annie—so he felt nothing.

Ahead some 500 yards, a dozen or so men of his infantry, his fightin' men from Texas, rested in the shade of apple trees at the end of the lane. They looked pitiful, as if they'd been living in a coal mine. Their skin was weather beaten and had the appearance of dull leather; some of them had no shoes, except for black rags wrapped around their feet.

Dwayne rode closer with his left hand on his hip and the other loosely holding Traveller's bridle. He gestured with his hand that was akimbo for the men to remain at ease as they started to get to their tattered feet upon spotting their beloved Uncle Robert headed their way. The men sat rigid as if at attention. One Rebel refused to stay down; he stood, removing his limp hat. The others stood with bare heads exposed to what is an April sun. Traveller stopped near the men on his own. Dwayne could not look them in their eyes until one of them said:

—General Lee, sir, we keep fightin' if you says so.

All the men grumbled in agreement and all were crying. Their faces were crimson from the emotions stored from a thousand days of unbearable hardships: all the lost comrades; ten thousand miles of marching and privations in every kind of weather; starvation so bad that they scraped the blood off crackers found on dead Yankees and ate them; and, the worst part of it, the endless waiting. The waiting had been for this day, the end of their fighting when they could return to their homes and families. He could see what these men were fighting for, and it was not some way of life that kept slavery alive or some provincial lifestyle. They fought for each other, and that was family. The real Robert E. Lee was the patriarch of that rebellious family. They believed that the wise old man would lead them to victory.

Dwayne had to move on. He was not here to be the general. He was here to see a lesson, something he must learn in order to live and become a writer/in; in some way immortalized like Lee, except D. H. Dayne wanted to live forever by having his books standing on library shelves in the cities and towns of his country; his words, insights and stories—all there to be read and imagined, just as the lives of Lee and Grant.

But then: Traveller, as if sensing his rider wanted to be away from company, sauntered away, toward and down a dusty road. In this powerful motion made from Traveller's steady gait, Dwayne thought of his proud brother, how Johnny had come to and left this earth without notice to most of the world. And that writing about him can only keep him alive in a literal sense, for Dwayne would never know what his proud brother was going through in those final hours of his surrender.

Now: he would know. Dwayne felt so weary. This pain in his chest must be Uncle Robert's aching heart. He wanted to stop Traveller and rest against one of the scrub apple trees or under the umbrageous boughs of a large apple tree not far off.

And then an aide of Lee's came galloping up to him on horseback, saying in an excited Southern drawl:

—Sir, General Grant is coming.

Dwayne followed his aide back to the McClean House. Dwayne looked around in the saddle for Ann as Grant and his entourage approached on horseback down the lane some fifty yards away. Consciously Dwayne tried to forget all he'd read about Appomattox. Lee's aides gathered around Traveller on foot with tattered sentries waiting on the front porch of the McClean House.

—Should protocol require you arrive after General Grant, sir? an aide asked Dwayne.

—We'll arrive together, he answered.

Now the slow hooves of Grant's party neared. Dwayne wished he knew his next move, for he did not have the mind of Robert E. Lee or pretend to know it. Grant's staff obscured Dwayne's vision of the famous general Dwayne was anxious to see more than anyone. When Grant got close enough, Dwayne knew why he was here. Grant's eyes were the Carolina-blue eyes of his brother John.

It was Dwayne who suggested they dismount and walk alone before they discuss terms. It didn't matter to Dwayne if this was not really part of history—he wanted privacy with his brother now disguised in a dusty blue coat of an enlisted man.

When they were out of hearing distance from anyone, Dwayne looked at Grant's dusty profile as they walked slowly, and big brother said:

—You must've known Mom would find you.

There was no answer from the man he was certain was his dead brother; then, Grant spoke with the voice of the boy Johnny:

—They started calling me Grant The Butcher after Cold Harbor. It was your skill as a strategist that prolonged the war. In reality, an argument can be made that Lee was more responsible for many more casualties than Grant...if you really think about it.

—You didn't answer my question.

—Things aren't as they seem. I was suffering in my mind

beyond what you or Mom knew. It was my pain. I chose to
d it.

ey stopped walking and faced one another from three feet away,
aring into the eyes of brothers beyond the battles between them.

—I'm sorry brother Dwayne...for all the pain my death
used you and our family. I love you.

ey cried and embraced. Then Dwayne asked his brother who
an Bruin is. As they separated and headed back toward the
cClean House, John told Dwayne:

—That's your girl, John smiled.

—My girl? What do you mean?

—Go to The Wilderness at night...you'll see, John smirked
his brother.

en: this sloppily dressed Yankee in dusty blue with the stout/
tle body and face of Grant, yet the eyes of brother John, said to
s brother in a hushed voice that was the raspy high pitch of boy
hnny:

—Brother Dwayne...you must know that life as you know
.is an illusion. Our meeting was a dream...though dreams are
al. Brother Dwayne...I was afraid before I left this world. I
ayed for peace a thousand times. I am at peace now.

—Can you go to Mom like this? She's in so much pain,
hnny. Why come to me and not her?

—That's not up to me. I would if I could.

—Why can't ya?

fore another word was said, it was over. Again, Dwayne found
mself on the ground in the Appomattox parking lot. It was back
the present with Traveller parked near Dwayne. He got to his
t. His legs were his again. He looked around for Ann. No sign
her or her car. He felt like hurling his guts out, because he was
ck to the present. And his brother was right: it was like a
eam—just when you want to know the important answer, it
nishes and ends at the penultimate moment.

Behind Traveller's wheel, he headed east on 460, three hours from Fredericksburg. For the entire drive, he thought of how all the people he knew who lead productive lives lived in the present with a dead past. The past had destroyed his brother. It was so clear to him now that his brother's looking back at his past mistakes, regrets, a thousand little things that kept him fearful of facing the future or risk-taking after a fall—destroyed him.

—She must've put something...

Then he remembered his brother telling him to go to The Wilderness at night. And that she's my girl. Did he mean the bloody battle at Spotsylvania? And if she drugged me, why bother he mused. Then he knew:

—The Bloody Angle, he whispered.

The concrete corridor up 95 was a maelstrom of metal on heels shooting north and south. And, for D. H. Dayne, closing in 1 Fredericksburg at night was especially thrilling. Since a boy, he anted to wake up early and stand atop Mayre's Hill and gaze wn on the scene at that battle. He had imagined it a thousand nes after reading about Lee's one-sided victory at Fredericksurg.

To stand atop that hill was a dream Dwayne had years fore his dying aunt told him he was related to Lee. He thought out how during the end of Gettysburg, when Uncle Robert ust've thought the terrible advantage he had atop Mayre's Hill d been reversed.

When he was here a decade ago, he met a girl who detracked his every thought pattern: Alissa. He was so enthralled ith her—he didn't have time for anything else.

As he cruised Traveller slowly down the two-way street that d downtown, he recalled that Fredericksburg is a dark place at ght in October. Its cinnamon/black brick streets appear as if they e the same matter used to build the stately homes of the historical ty. The street lights cast a shadowy/yellow pall that brings down e light, matching the yellow on sister Karen's chart for past es/family.

The library was easy to find in this winter gloom, since he as a patron here ten years ago. He remembered he told Ann that would be here for his first book signing from Karen's chart.

Driving Traveller along the narrow streets and short blocks th traffic signals in downtown Fredericksburg was like sliding a eadbox on an ironing board. Traveller's wheels waffled on the

-133-

cobblestone surface of the town's main drag.

Yes, the Fredericksburg Library was still there, after some 200 years. The benches were still there in front before the steps leading up to the library. He had kissed Alissa on one of those benches.

The parking lot was small; he parked lengthwise near the sidewalk so he could exit easily. There would be no problem parking here for a couple of nights; he'd make sure it was okay with the librarian tomorrow morning. His book signing was the day after tomorrow, about 48 hours from now.

After he locked Traveller, he walked briskly; he was headed to the heart of the city with his black leather folder that held his clean white paper with no lines and two pencils, sharp and each pencil ready to replace the other. He was going back to Sammy's Restaurant and Bar, his favorite place to write while having a good meal with good fresh coffee. He looked forward to seeing the walnut booth tables that were high-backed and conducive to long spans of writing and conversation. And inside Sammy's, the lighting was soft with a very high ceiling. Perfect for writing, he ruminated.

Fredericksburg is a walking-man's town, with enough of a rolling pitch to give a good workout after an hour or two. He would walk from one side of town to the other, prowling day and night five miles away from his apartment in either direction.

But this stretch was flat. He quickened his pace into the roar of river wind gusts coming and going; gusts that were whipping the town's incredible trees into a frenzy, stripping million of brittle leaves, blow after blow, adding up to a maelstrom of clittering, a sound made only in autumn where the Rapidan River rushed beside.

The sky was cloud-covered in blackness. Yes, glorious winter was in the air, flaring his nostrils so clean and alive, as he passed the sparkling retail shops of a truly historical American bur

He always felt the presence of colonial days in Fredericksburg. And it wasn't just because of the buildings and streets; it was in the air. Fredericksburg air was always charged with some electric vibrance that brought great men and women, and great armies here. He could hear the Rapidan River to his left, as it carried away the last wave of dead summer pollen.

Those Fredericksburg trees, colorless now at night, resplendent in light because of a quick/short freeze two weeks ago; they kept up their roar along his route, the tops of these great trees swaying like graceful dancers—back and forth—and then holding in gust before letting go of but a few of its goldenrod leaves that floated to the bricks of Fredericksburg.

D. H. Dayne knew he would write about Alissa now. By the time he reached Sammy's he was anxious to pour her from his left hand onto whiteness. He had walked faster the last hundred yards. He felt free for the first time in a very long time. Was it a surrender, a letting go of his brother's death at Appomattox? he wondered. Or, was it part of some willingness 'to see" his brother and forgive him and himself? After all: he had seen his brother again, even if it was an illusion, a dream, hallucination, whatever. Before he stepped into Sammy's warm atmosphere he noticed how his body felt free and loose, his arms and legs moving without the usual stiffness, uneasiness.

Was it due to the fact he now had hope alive again in his life? What would he find in The Wilderness...at night? Alissa had lived in Spotsylvania. At least I'm alive and able to write another time:

I sat at my favorite table, the same booth I sat in that day in late January, in Sammy's Restaurant on the corner of Washington and Main in Fredericksburg.

Every man has a day he remembers fondly, a day when an unforgettable woman comes into his life and gives him the spark he needs to be truly alive.

I thought I was successful then, with twenty women in the South working from their homes for me, telemarketing to local businesses for a local chiropractor. For once, I had money saved in the bank after a long drought in scarcity. So, I was able to write every day and eat a good meal in Sammy's. It was right when I hit forty that I looked and felt successful.

I had been churning to approach and pitch the first attractive woman I saw, but most times...I chickened out, or found something specious about them, and I'd end up bitter and alone, again, while going for a long walk. I had the habit of writing in the morning when I had coffee, and in the evening when my marketing to D.C.'s and training new girls on the phone was done. I usually managed to write something every time I sat down to do so.

I missed many opportunities, I know, to meet new women, because I was writing up a storm. But this meeting at Sammy's would be the luckiest day in my life in many ways.

I was at this very table, in a space of readiness to flirt when I saw her crossing the street, headed toward Sammy's front door with two friends. Her skin-tight jeans revealed a 5'4" tanned pistol of a body that made Sammy's disappear entirely. Her brindle colored hair was short with long flat bangs hiding her brow as she stepped quickly inside from the January cold. I said:

—Hey.

And she returned one. We both were not inclined to smile big or pretend to. I can still see that body walking to the restroom. That's when I overheard from her table just across the aisle but back one: "Arizona." I told her friends that I was from Phoenix; and one of her friends said that Alissa was from Phoenix.

—Oh, yeah, I smiled, with a grin that had to look like the Cheshire Cat himself.

When Alissa returned to her table, before she sat down, I told her I was from Phoenix. She came right over to my table and stood there, looking down at me with those black/brown eyes. I liked her because she didn't ask me what I do for a living. She gave me her phone number and I gave her mine. I remembered thinking that it was all too easy. My wise old Grampa Hutch used to warn me with his sightless blue eyes ablaze:

—Be careful when a girl is easy...because she sees something she wants...and can get easily.

But I didn't care about that. I remember watching her tan body leaving Sammy's, and I couldn't help from staring at her muscular buns, firm to perfection, in those tight designer jeans from Scottsdale.

I even recall walking home after meeting her. My mind had changed from tired-eyed phone slug to imageries of romantic hand-holding walks along the Rapidan sidewalk lined with hardwood pines.

I kept going over her essence in my mind; she had that vibrancy of a tough/independent chick who could blow a man's mind if she liked him. My mind looked forward to it.

Two days later: I called Alissa, and before I could ask her out, my call-waiting beeped. I knew it was a money call—a chiropractor wanting to talk about my service. I told Alissa I'd have to call her back. But she called me back the minute I finished with the doctor. Boy, was that refreshing for a change. I liked that about Alissa: aggressive and confident. Tomorrow we'd have our first date.

I chose a late lunch at a restaurant with a view of the river, not far from the Amtrak station. I was smart enough to walk there, not wanting her to see Lawn Boy, my blue Hyundai, on our first date. After all, I hadn't written *Ledges* yet, so I couldn't impress a doctor's daughter who lived in Spotsylvania in her father's million-dollar home.

Just then: Dwayne dropped his pencil. He realized what was going on with Appomattox, the spinning back, the holding onto dogwoods, his brother, The Wilderness, and Annie. It was all so clear now. He picked up his pencil and wrote:

I know now that Gene in *Ledges*, Harvey/Floyd in *The Paper Man*, and J. D. in *Missouri Madness* had all resolved past trauma in their cells that were circulating in their blood. This "spinning back" that happens to me...is all related to being in the right place to relive past trauma in order to make room for a peaceful death and a much better life in the present. This is all so real and interesting to me that I truly do look forward to every new day, though the pain can be incredible to bear, an emotional pain that's hard to describe. I want joy to come from this willingness to see. Maybe that's what joy is—the willingness to let go of the past

Then: he continued writing about his date with Alissa:

On the crisp walk to the riverfront restaurant, my eyes focused away from the manmade things: traffic; the old buildings; the Fredericksburg stone streets I crossed; the time ticking on my wrist. This was some phantasmal sense of movement to a beautiful woman who anticipated his return to her. My eyes could see the Eastern Redbud trees with their heart-shaped foliage, their once magenta pink flowers now purplish black, and to the background of the exploding sassafras with its orange and scarlet leaves shimmering their tiny rivulets in unceasing winds of untraceable sound that only lovers hear.

I never felt more alive in my life, anticipating meeting her. My beard was full with a little gray. I felt like Uncle Robert's vigor was running through me; my legs felt light and my step so quick. And it was Lee's birthday tomorrow. I wanted to go to Stratford, his birthplace, and walk the grounds of the man I heard I was related to on my mother's side, and whose image taped to my wall in front of my phone, gave me strength daily, a stamina to endure when I wanted to quit. Yes, I will go tomorrow on his birthday—whether or not Alissa goes with me.

Alissa was right on time. I stood back some fifty feet from the front door, near our private table overlooking the river. She looked happy to see me without smiling; her walk over to me was athletic and fast as if in a hurry.

For an instant: Dwayne left his writing at Sammy's to dwell on the words his brother told him about going to The Wilderness at night. His brother never knew that Alissa lived near The Wilderness battlefield in Spotsylvania. What will I see there? he wondered, then he picked up his pencil and continued writing about Alissa:

After our late lunch, it was getting dark and cold. My idea was to board the train to D.C., an hour ride at the most.

We sat close together, oblivious to the lights in darkness shooting by our window. I asked her about her family and found out that her mother killed herself when Alissa was a little girl. She talked about her mother's habit at night of tucking in her daughter's covers and saying, "Sweet dreams...and snazzy squirrels." I can still see her telling me this poignant memory, her slight lisp so soft on her bottom lip; but I remember that I was unable to really connect with her by looking deep into her eyes; she wouldn't go here.

Again: Dwayne stopped moving his pencil and thought about how he had created Josie in *The Paper Man* from Alissa's childhood. How else can a writer stay connected and validate his life as a writer if he does not consciously remember and write about those characters in his life, until they live forever on paper, there for all to see, yet never truly knowing just how writing is never fiction, and truly is connected in organic flashes of love, memory and all the senses—real or imagined.

Back to Alissa: After revealing herself so matter-of-factly, she was searching for some humor, a way out of this moment, from this man to whom she was attracted.

In Washington, we walked in the bitter cold passing government buildings. My brown trench coat kept me warm yet unstylish to her. Looking back, I believe I'd rather have been cold and stylish in her eyes.

Then, I stopped her on the sidewalk along a row of cherry trees across from the Capitol Building. Until then, I had only held her gloved hand in mine. I felt it was good timing to kiss her, so I opened my cheap coat and pulled her close to me, wrapping its lining around her. The kiss and motion in her hips made me want her all the way back to Fredericksburg. We were both in the throes of a sexual drought and were chased away by a security guard like dogs in heat at the Supreme Court Building when we were caught making out behind a column in the shadows of the hallowed building while sharing my coat. I cannot remember a word we spoke, but we laughed hard after we were chased off the property. I think she was laughing at my coat.

On the train home, I had two shots of Jack Daniels and that was when she told me that her father is an alcoholic, an eye doctor who's now living with his second wife in their beautiful home in Spotsylvania. She said that she'd been living there for three months since moving from Arizona.

We kissed a lot for most of the ride back to Fredericksburg; I rode in her car to my place. I felt lucky.

My apartment was in an upstairs brownstone on Pitt Street, a block from the river. As we climbed the narrow carpeted stairway I had no idea I was following a storm, a storm named

Alissa. I could tell from our pieces of conversation and the silence between them, that I was not commandeering at all what I really wanted to say, only that something special was about to happen. Yes, she would be a visual memory for me, much longer than most girls I'd dated.

For some reason, I felt she was untouchable to love... because...I was. And this is what goes and comes 'round again after I had been the one to not love a woman who loved me.

She liked the independent way I lived. She stood in my warm kitchen office under the low sloping ceiling by my desk near a small window. She scanned the taped three-dozen 3 x 5 cards on the wall, each one a file on a chiropractic client on my service. When her brown eyes went to the photo of Uncle Robert on Traveller in Petersburg near the end of the war:

—He's my inspiration. I'm related to him.

No response.

—It's his birthday tomorrow. Would you like to go to his plantation with me tomorrow? They have a restaurant there. It's only about thirty miles from here.

—I can't. I've got plans tomorrow.

I just nodded okay.

I have no recollection of the music I played in my studio apartment that first night with Alissa. My vision of her dulled other senses that made me as invisible as dust mites. I'm not one to kiss and tell or describe sexual things, but three things are haunting about the girl Alissa I call Stormy. These things stick with me from a maleness point of view and are dismissed as trivial to women, I suppose: No. 1—the way she looked when she stood by my floor mattress in her plum-colored silk panties and bra after removing her slacks and sweater. She stood there for me, giving my sore eyes a gift they will never forget. To describe her figure would offend most women of Puritan mind. All I'll say is that she was 5'4 of the best toned body I'd ever laid eyes on. No. 2—she was afraid to let go, all the way, falling in love. I know this is true because so was I. No. 3—my big mouth. During sex, while in a new position (for me) that was incredible, I called her "circus lady."

That was the end of our first date. The next day, I found myself at Lee's birthplace thinking about Stormy. Oh, how the circus lady stormed out of my apartment. I knew it was just a good excuse for her to leave without intimacy.

Yes, Alissa had made most of the late morning so lonely while roaming around the beautiful grounds of Stratford. I kept thinking about her while standing among happy couples touring Lee's house with its many small rooms and bits of history as told by the tour guide. In the ballroom, with its high ceiling and open double doors that opened on each side of the room exposing green expansive lawns, I imagined General Washington dancing in this very room while two dozen slaves toiled in the tobacco fields within view.

I broke away from the tour, going upstairs after seeing the room where Robert E. Lee was born. I stood at the top of the house on a circular observation deck, bathing my eyes in the ordered austerity I could see all around me. And even now, the circus lady was on my mind. She had talked about how people label people, pre-judge them and slap their label on lesbian, homo, Jew, old guy, old lady. Then, I went back to my stupid comment when I labeled her a circus lady. I meant it to be funny, to get her to laugh, for she was struggling to hold onto something when we were so close.

I wondered if I'd ever see her again, because she was so upset when she stormed out. I could see me holding her, with my arms around her while standing up here behind her; my chin would be touching the back of her lush chocolate/auburn hair, and I would smell that sweet scent of her hair.

He stopped writing and removed the vile of joy essential oil rom his pocket. Dwayne removed the cap and took in a deep whiff f the oil Ann gave him. His face relaxed more with each xhalation, then he dabbed a drop of the oil under his nostrils. oon, he was thinking that there are ways to let go of things that eople do to you. Edgar Cayce was the one that said that most of is patients' illnesses were caused by poor eliminations. I believe hese things damage us emotionally; they are things that emote from he heart and the brain, and manifest to billions of cells that irculate in the blood, giving us the very chemistry of who we are nd what we become. Imageries should be positive and charged vith such vivid colors that construct a cell structure conducive to ustaining good health. If that's too hard for you, Dwayne: Cry.

I continued writing:

Even without Alissa here at Stratford...I feel like my life is ood. I can remember thinking that. I then realized I was thinking bout my writing as I tramped down the cement steps that brought ie level with the expansive Stratford grounds. I headed for the ow of little shacks where the slaves lived, some three hundred ards off, under the grayest of skies. How fitting it should be such gray day on his birthday, I mused. Could this truly be my great reat grandfather's place of birth? I so wanted to be related to him, hough if he were here today and I a relation, he'd give me a good alkin'-to about my bad habits—for sure. I'd rather believe I am elated and have this Lee pride in my will and consciousness that he ustains in me.

As I approached the plaintive shacks of hundreds of stolen ouls, I realized I needed writing and Uncle Robert to give me lentity. What am I without my precious readers? I am not an ducated writer from the classroom. I am an experimental writer vho wants to hold the storyline interest for thousands of readers, iostly women, women who follow my characters to places I've been. Like here at Stratford—and at Sammy's:

Dwayne stuck his hand into the concealed back pocket of his black leather writing folder that he called Blacky. It was a hiding place where he stashed a black and white photo of his father with his father in the early 1940's.

Also, he found an old letter from a retired Iowa English teacher who read *Ledges* and *Missouri Madness*. The letter read: Mr. Dayne: Do you remember compound and complex sentences from your high school English courses? Your writing would be much more professional if you would vary your sentence structure. For example: look at the first paragraph on page 32 of *Missouri Madness*. Notice how repetitious your sentences are, mostly simple sentences beginning with "he." How about this instead?

Dwayne skipped over her suggestion, smiling at how this teacher, so pedantic, and how he's able to dismiss her critique without penalty or guilt; he reads on:

Do you write on a word processor or a computer, Mr. Dayne? If not, and I guess your manuscript must have been typewritten, judging by underlined words; you must invest in a computer. An aspiring writer cannot be without one. Also, go to a bookstore and get a book of synonyms; you will need one. A book of punctuation rules is also necessary.

He knew that was enough of that bullshit. He folded her letter, jammed it inside Blacky's back pocket and sat back on Sammy's hardwood booth. He grumbled on, thinking about the teacher's advice and how she had made him want to explain to her just how much he abhorred "proper" grammar and how he hated explaining himself to anybody. And, teacher, that's why I'm self-published. My writing is not good enough for the publishing world's agents, editors, and gawd-damn English teachers. Half the people in the world can't even read. Maybe that's my audience,

teacher. Go teach them how to read, how to use your rules of
proper grammar; it's your properness that keeps ten million like me
afraid to come out and knock on your door "properly," to put their
work out there, to risk themselves incredibly without knowing
rules, without having your validation, teacher. Well, I will use my
typewriter, teacher, because it is slow and forces me to be more
accurate. And because I like the sound of its humming motor, and
the strike of each letter that makes the blackness of words scream
out the words like HE! HE! HE! HE!

He continued writing:

As I neared the Stratford slave quarters, I thought of other
letters I'd received. One, in particular, was from a librarian in
Robert Lee, Texas, where Captain R. E. Lee was stationed prior to
the Civil War. The librarian returned his books because she said
they were not good enough for her patrons.

After ducking into the slave shacks, observing the worn
spartan wood furnishings and scrubbed-raw pine floors, I imagined
my rejection letters on these walls, though my wall of rejection
tales in comparison to the pains and hardships endured by the poor
souls who lived between these walls, walls that I could see had been
scrubbed clean to sandpaper smoothness during twenty-thousand
days and nights of abject poverty, the likes of which I had never
known and never will. These people must have known they were
poor. My family didn't.

Outside: I stayed with my breath, in the moment, resisting
the urge to go back to my childhood. My sister Karen is a pro
regarding the past. She said she could research our genealogical
lineage to Lee. I told her I wasn't ready to know. I'd let her know
when I was ready to know.

Even now, as I head for the restaurant to have a good lunch
alone, I remembered thinking about my sister. So, I returned my

focus to my breath and the Stratford surroundings. I saw more cabins. But these were bigger cabins, nicer, and stained a burnt red They were for guests of the Daughters of the Confederacy, those members who donated money to the foundation that keeps Marse Robert's spirit alive.

The vast screened-in dining area was open, offering a magnificent view of Virginia wilderness that was covered with thin stands of hardwoods mostly.

Alone, again I thought of sweet Alissa and how incredibly romantic it would be if she were here to share this lovely table with me.

An elderly waitress took my order; she was a spinster-looking woman adorned in a gray ankle-length cotton dress with an embroidered apron that cursively spelled Daughters of the Confederacy in red letters. Just then:

I broke away from Stratford and wrote down this poem about my experience at Appomattox I titled
"Shy Ann"
she was behind me
all the way,
until Appomattox
where gray surrendered to blue,
I awakened as Lee
in a mist of green
until Johnny's call
from the porch of McClean,
we went inside
to discuss our sin,
and came out united
brothers again.

Dwayne continued writing:

After that delightful lunch at Stratford, I drove to my apartment on Pitt Street. Alissa's car was parked in front of my place. I can remember feeling the explosive rush of seeing her again as I hurried up to my apartment to catch her, but neither she nor a note was at my door.

Outside, I looked around and hustled for the boardwalk at the end of Pitt Street. I marched west into the sun beside the rippling river after I'd left a brochure from Stratford on her windshield, since she didn't know Lawn Boy.

It was just warm enough to keep my hands and feet from freezing if I kept walking. Barren branches of gray Willows and Mulberries were heavy to my right along the riverbank laden with scrubs of dead blue chicory and purple crown vetch.

I walked as fast as my hips would move, seeing nobody for the first mile or so. A hundred times I walked this path alone, seeing happy couples hand-in-hand. Oh, how I wanted her hand in mine at that instant.

Just when I began to think she may have walked to downtown Fredericksburg, perhaps to Sammy's: she came into view, 200 yards ahead and coming toward me on the sidewalk. She was wearing a maroon jogging outfit; her walking shoes were bright white and closing. We waved at the same instant. A good sign, I thought. I could see her auburn bangs on her brown skin, a color she bought at a Fredericksburg tanning salon in order to keep her Arizona tan.

My mouth was dry and parched for hers, for I craved that kiss from her folded tongue so sweet and wet for passion. I hadn't felt this attracted to a woman since my roaring twenties. Now: I'm young again with these spontaneous whimsical flirtings bursting within. Just then: I could hear Floyd from my novel *The Paper Man* reminding me to let her be the first to speak. So, I waited, until only 50 yards of empty space was between us. I smiled and consciously breathed deeper to relax my throat that was constricting to reach her with a joyous greeting like: Hey, Alissa! I missed you, girl!

Instead, I listened to Floyd and kept quiet until I heard her sexy greeting:

—I came to track you down.

I brought her into my chest and kissed her mouth with the last bit of a mint from Stratford on my tongue. We held the kiss for many seconds. I can remember consciously thinking that I will always remember this kiss. After the kiss, yet close to her mouth, our eyes wide open, I whispered her nickname:

—Stormy.

She laughed at the name, not at all wondering why I called her Stormy. She knew. It was much more to her liking compared to circus lady.

I headed us back toward Pitt Street, taking her hand in mine as we walked fast. Her hand squeezed hard, not at all tender or holding back, but firm—like her body, ready for action.

She didn't ask me where I'd been, so I told her about Stratford, how incredible the place is. It didn't interest her. I had this feeling that she wanted to be with me...to find out something. I so wanted to tell her about how I felt at the slave quarters at Stratford. And how being there pushed out of me this feeling of despair and rejection I get from my writing. I wanted so much to tell her that it was the thought of her that pulled me out of it, away from a thousand words of unwelcome criticism and callous rejection from some jowl-flapping educated haybag. Yet, all the negative was wiped away into stillness with just the hope of holding her hand and getting a squeeze from those same little fingers that lost everything so long ago when her mother took her own life.

And I wanted to pin her right there on the dead grass, and scream into her face that I would write about her one day in one of my novels. That she would be Harvey's "young girl" Josie, who would fall in love with a paper man, a toilet paper salesman who worshiped and adored her; he was The Paper Man, the lovesick salesman who kept her dream alive...by saying nothing.

Then: I would fall onto her chest, and she would hold me and tell me I'll be okay if I ever lose someone close to me. She will tell me how to get over it. She will tell me a thousand things she did to keep herself from hurting and missing her so. She will let me feel that it's safe, safe to cry into her face, and let me pour out my grief onto her tan skin, skin that covers a thousand places to give me comfort. She will understand. She will love me. She will laugh with me when I play "Stormy" from my Classics IV CD. She! She! She! She!

But then: I gushed, a block from my apartment:

—I've been thinkin' about you all day.

No reply. The voice of Floyd was telling me to shut up, though Harvey, Floyd's romantic and sensitive alter ego was winning:

—I'm sorry I hurt your feelings last night when I called you circus lady. That was stupid. I'm sorry. Alissa laughed a courtesy laugh that said "forget it." When Alissa talked, she talked fast, with a trace of an adorable lisp, like that of an anxious girl:

—I had breakfast with Jennifer, my friend you met at Sammy's. She's upset because she's off work today and wanted me to spend the day with her.

—Uh huh, I said, ignoring Floyd's needs.

—She's so into control and always wants her way, Alissa continued as our walk slowed a bit when we reached Pitt Street. My big mouth again:

—I know we've only had one date, and I don't know your friend Jennifer. I cannot discuss her problems or listen to them as a friend who knows her. I just want to spend time getting to know you right now, okay?

Later, after I relieved myself, alone, I played my Classics IV CD, listening to "Stormy" while thinking of the storm that drove away mad a second time in less than a 24-hour period.

Angel of Mercy

Dwayne dropped his pencil, checked his wrist watch; it was
near closing at Sammy's and he wasn't tired. He decided when
walking back to Traveller that he would drive Lawn Boy to The
Wilderness as his brother said. Alissa's father's house was on the
way near the battlefield, but, no, he would certainly not drive by
after no contact with his daughter for so many years, he told himself
mordantly.

Her father's house was very hard to find at night, because it
was hard to find in the daytime. He drove Lawn Boy down the
long winding paved road named Angle Road, off the main road
deep into the woods on the fringe of The Wilderness in
Spotsylvania.

—What am I doing here? he groaned in self deprecation,
since it had been seven long years since he'd seen her.

Her father's name was still on the mailbox. At least he
knew he could call him and find out what she's up to. Maybe, he
thought.

Dwayne turned his mind and Lawn Boy toward The
Wilderness, knowing something was coming, something was
coming related to his brother, Ann, Alissa, Uncle Robert, or all of
them—whatever; some lesson, perhaps, about to be revealed under
his harvest moon that was cream-colored and ominous as only in
October.

Even if this turned out to be a big waste of time, at least his
little brother's words about The Wilderness were not dismissed.
Dwayne still had no idea just how he ended up on the ground at
Appomattox; he would welcome the same thing here if it came.

The main road that led to the main Battlefield National Park from Spotsylvania was narrow and winding, a portentous blue/gray in the luminous moonlight. Then Dwayne looked in Lawn Boy's rear-view mirror to see if he was aging or re-youthing as at Appomattox. No change. But then: when the entrance to the park was within a mile or less: Dwayne's legs began to tremble. Again, he looked in the mirror and saw no change on his face.

The exact spot where Stonewall Jackson was mortally wounded was within a hundred yards of the park entrance. A gate was blocking his way into the park, so he parked outside the gate, but off to the side—not so obvious if park rangers saw his car. Then, his legs began to tremble, bad, like a dog shittin' razor blades.

He could see The Wilderness trail maps behind several glass historical markers that were lit all along the parking area. The moon's light made the maps easy to read without straining. His finger shivered as it slid along the glass, quaking with his legs when his finger stopped at a spot on the map; it was a spot just across the parking area via a trail Yankees entered on the way to the battle that would be named Bloody Angle.

In the glass: He thought of how he'd been here before, not the time that he lived here and met Alissa, but rather in a past life, perhaps, in that spring of 1864, that terrible spring.

Again: he looked at his reflection in the glass historical marker. No change. Except: he could see a copy of a letter written by General Lee to his wife about the time of this battle. Dwayne began to read the letter from Lee out loud:

—I cannot express the anguish I feel at the death of our sweet Annie. To know that I shall never see her again on earth, that her place in our circle, which I always hoped one day to enjoy, is forever vacant, is agonizing to the extreme. But God in this, as in all things, has mingled mercy with the blow in selecting that one best prepared to leave us... When I reflect on all she will escape in life, brief and painful at the best...I cannot wish her back.

Now: after reading Lee's letter about Annie, he was going
wn again, as at Appomattox Dwayne was soon on the parking lot
ment caught in some numinous spinning back in time. In a fetal
sition he screamed for the world to stop spinning, this merry-go-
und that was moving counter-clockwise. This time the colors
re different; they were a blood red mixed with swirling black.
e knew that black meant 'the mind" on Karen's chart. But, he
dn't know that red was on the chart. Then: he lost conscious-
ss.

Before Dwayne opened his eyes, he could smell smoke from
rning timber and leaves. Then, the pathetic plaintive cries of men
rning alive was off in the darkness. When he opened his eyes, the
d and black were there in the dark woods around him. He looked
wn his body and could see he was now wearing the tattered
othes of a Rebel private.

—In Lee's army, his whispered to himself.

The air was warmer now. He sat up, whereupon he could
e Rebel pickets, a small group of Rebel infantrymen lying about
d sitting behind abatis made up of branches mostly blown down
om artillery fire. Just then: a distinct Southern voice from the
uster of men warned him:

—Better getcher head down, boy..."fore it's gone!"

Again, there was the sad and desperate wailing of wounded
d thirsty men caught in brush fires coming from the dense thicket
tangled brush in all directions. A man's screams while burning
ve caused Dwayne to scramble to his feet and run, crouched
er, to the Rebels of the Third Arkansas.

The thought of his Yankee accent stopped him from asking
y questions. He could plainly see that all of the men around him
d "devil moons" for eyes—scared eyes that shone bright from the
cent carnage seen in battle.

A ragged Rebel with permanent neck dirt came over to
wayne. The man smelled bad, real bad; he offered Dwayne some

roasted rat and dog meat on a stick.

Dwayne declined the offer.

—Where you from, boy?

—Asheville, Dwayne answered in a soft drawl.

The man grunted and said:

—Them Yanks are gettin' a twenty-devil whippin'.

Down the line Dwayne could hear two men talking about the death of Lee's daughter. They disagreed over how old Annie was. One said sixteen; the other said no, she was thirteen.

Now: the screams from the dying men increased as flashes of fire would grow here and there. Some of the wounded men could be seen moving deep into the thickets. Dwayne remembered to use a Southern accent when he asked the men:

—Ain't there s'posed to be some sort of truce between the lines to get the wounded out?

—Grant or Lee won't call one.

—Why not? Dwayne asked.

—Whoever asks first...admits to losin' the battle.

Dwayne forgot his accent and his surroundings when he exclaimed:

—Everything I've read about Lee says he's such a compassionate man. I can't believe he'd let those men suffer! The Rebels laughed at the man's ignorance until a ragged old soldier without teeth told Dwayne:

—Them's Yankees out there.

Just then: as Dwayne turned to the dying pleas for water coming from the dark woods, he remembered something from his reading. His thoughts went into a whirlwind: Lee's letter about his daughter Annie; the angel of mercy he'd read about, a mysterious Rebel maiden who brought the wounded Yankees fresh milk in The Wilderness. Could Annie be Shy Ann, a slave girl he wrote about so long ago? Could Ann, who came to him at Dixieland, the abandoned baby girl he pledged to help from his book sales, could she have been Lee's daughter the angel of mercy who died so

oung? And, if I'm related to Lee...has Ann Bruin come back as
he abandoned girl whose beloved father left her to go to war?

Trance-like, Dwayne stood up and walked unarmed toward
he pitiful cries for help coming from the thickets in front of him.

—Hey, boy! Get back here! the toothless picket barked.

Dwayne ignored the calls for him to return and soon
anished in the woods. The woods brought more darkness though
e could see discarded canteens, rifles and haversacks left behind by
fleeing army. He gathered canteens and looped them over his
houlder as he dodged barbed brush on his crouch forward toward
he wailing wounded.

There were brambles of buckthorn shrubs with spiny
ranches. Their fruit on its leaves looked like blackberries. Horse
hestnuts fifty feet tall and American birch over three hundred years
ld, just earlier today spreading shade, now spread suffering with
:s artillery-downed dry branches, fueling flames to the wounded via
Queen Ann's lace, dandelions and hawkweed.

This reminded him of how he was spared seeing combat
uring the war in Viet Nam when he was in the service, and how he
lways felt protected from seeing the horror of war. Just then: on
he other side of a deep ditch with grassy lips and once tree-tufted
lopes, a wounded Yankee lay near the trunk of a small tree riddled
vith shot. The man had his blue shirt raised above his bare belly
hat had a gaping hole that the poor young man covered with his
ands, concealing his exposed red intestines. The wounded man
ad a sweaty mouth that had black powder smudges from bitten
artridges.

Dwayne knelt and poured water from a canteen over the
lying man's lips. The Yankee's blazing blue eyes were so
rightened and thankful as the dying man prayed incoherently.

He left the canteen for the man and continued on; soon he
tumbled upon two dead soldiers charred to a black crisp after
eing wounded and burned alive after stripping themselves of their

clothes.

Further on, into what seemed an interminable tangle of brush and wilderness, another wounded man in dusty blue was left canteen beside his shattered thigh. Dwayne could see the outline of yellow cream or milk stained around the wounded man's parched lips. Dwayne asked the man if he'd seen who brought him milk. No answer. When Dwayne left, he saw that the wounded man had a cocked pistol at his side, ready to use on himself if fire came his way. Somehow Dwayne knew that this had something to do with his own brother taking his life.

Soon, compassion began to overtake him, welling up his eyes; and then he was sobbing again as he had when he was clutching the dogwood while Ann waited in the Blackstone restaurant just before Appomattox.

Smoke from burning brush was getting thicker and burning the hell out of his tearing eyes. He looked down at his hands that were blackened and stained from gun powder. He touched his face that was scruffy as a bear with rough stubble all the way down his neck. Then, up ahead in a clearing, he saw the specter of a girl dressed in a white cotton dress; she was moving to and fro from one wounded man to another with her wooden pail of buttermilk. He hesitated before going after her, straining to see if this angel of mercy was Ann Bruin. He couldn't tell from where he was, for she wore a white bonnet that shielded her face. The front of her skirt was stained with blood, and he could see arms of blue reaching for her to comfort them with the rich buttermilk.

She turned his way when he coughed from the stifling smoke. He still couldn't be sure. As she looked his way:

—Ann? He called to her.

She stepped lightly his way, her face yet indistinguishable. Again he called:

—Is that you, Ann?

He tried to walk toward her, but his legs wouldn't move, as if

orbidden by some specter force to approach her. His legs trembled
bad he had to drop to his knees or fall down. Within some
wenty feet of him, he could hear her light step moving closer; then,
e fell back onto his rump and lay flat on his back with his legs bent
t his knees.

When she stood over him with her wooden ladle rubbing
gainst the inside of her pail, he could see her face. It wasn't Ann
ruin's face. He asked her:

—Do you know me?

he nodded no.

—Are you General Lee's Annie.

he didn't answer. She smiled and knelt beside him, ladling
uttermilk to his lips that he refused, by saying:

—No, please save it for the others.

When she took the ladle away, he touched her hand and asked her
ngelic face that was smeared in places from smoke and soot and
loody hands if she knew why he was here now. She smiled into
is eyes; the woods around him started spinning faster and faster,
lockwise, until Dwayne passed out.

Ms. Virginia

The Fredericksburg Library was crowded in the main meeting room. More than three dozen people were seated on folding chairs, curious to hear the self-published novelist D. H. Dayne. All of them had read all of his books. The library director, Mrs. Thistlethwaite, was waiting for her guest speaker near the front door; she's holding an e-mail message in her hand from Dwayne's sister Karen that read: Please have my brother D. H. Dayne check his e-mail from your location. Thank you, sister Karen.

Just when the elderly director was considering knocking on the writer's motor home door in her parking lot, Dwayne came inside the library carrying a case of his books on his shoulder. He was dressed up in slacks and sweater with dress shoes; his hair spiked evenly to the shape of his head.

—Mrs. Thistlethwaite! Hi! Or..Hey! Anybody show up? Dwayne smiled, his face glowing with confidence.

—Yes, there's quite a turnout for you, she said coldly while leading her guest author to the meeting room.

—I hope my sister told you that I don't read passages from my books at signings.

—Oh, that reminds me, your sister e-mailed me today to have you check your e-mail before you leave the library.

—Okay, he said upon entering the crowded, yet quiet, meeting room.

When Dwayne reached the podium at the front of the room as Mrs. T. was about to introduce him: He couldn't believe his eyes when he saw Alissa, his old Fredericksburg flame, seated in the back row next to a heavyset, elderly black woman with gray hair. Alissa miled at his gaping mouth. She looked fantastic.

Dayne handed Mrs. T. a copy of his new book:

—Looks better, huh?

—How much are they?

—Twenty dollars each.

—I'll take two, she smiled.

—Great.

His mind was on Alissa when she introduced him:

—We are pleased to have as our guest the self-published ovelist D. H. Dayne, whose first three books have been circulating uite well in our library. With a show of hands, how many of you ave read any of Mr. Dayne's books?

Dwayne could see that nearly all in the audience raised a hand, ncluding Alissa, but not the black woman seated beside her. He hought that Alissa must be near 40 by now, and appeared to be in he same great shape. He wanted to go right over to her and ask ier a thousand things.

—Now, we'll let Mr. Dayne talk to his readers.

A smattering of applause made him smirk a bit as he stood at the podium without a mike.

—Thank you, he smiled, wanting to say thanks for nothin'. Ie could see Alissa covering her mouth to conceal her amusement rom the droll reception. Dwayne cleared his throat and said:

—It's good to be back in Fredericksburg. I lived here about even years ago.

Alissa's smile made him blush.

—Rather than ramble on about old stories, I'd like to talk bout my new book.

Ie showed them the front cover of his new title before giving a copy of it to a lady in the front row, adding:

—If you can please pass my new book around, you'll see hat it looks better than my other books.

Back at the podium:

—Why don't I answer any questions any of you may have...I hope.

Courtesy laughter, then, a middle-aged woman in the front row asked:

—Your books have interesting storylines, but they need quite a bit of editing. Why don't you have your books professionally edited?

—I'm an experimental writer. That means I think I know what I'm doing, but nobody else thinks I do.

More courtesy laughter from the audience, then Dwayne continued:

—When I self-published *Ledges*, my first book, I had no money—not a dime to spare for editing. So, with borrowed money, I had to sell *Ledges* with small print because I told my printer to shoot my pages camera-ready to keep the cost of the book down. I sold most of that first printing door-to-door to retail outlets: drugstores, grocery stores, independent bookstores, beauty shops, florists, and gift shops. And, I got back quite a few books, returned to me by those retailers because of the size of the print and the format—the way it looked. And most of them bought from me because I guaranteed to buy them back if they didn't sell. Anyway, on the second printing of *Ledges* I also had no money for editing because of heavy returns, and I ordered five thousand more copies; the same as the first printing. My second book *The Paper Man* had bigger font, but no margins or editing because I still had no money.

Before he continued, he could see Alissa listening intently at the back of the room.

—I'm a high school graduate. I flunked out of college without a credit. I have no concept regarding rules of proper grammar. But I do know how to tell a story. I'm a screenwriter who turned my scripts into novels. My goal is to take my novels straight to video. And that takes money.

Another raised hand asked:

—Your books are as good as many out there. Why can't

ou get a publisher?

  —Most publishers and agents dismiss self-published
riters...for going around them...out of the loop. I do better than
ost writers, because most writers don't get published.
nother question:

  —I heard that you sell your book directly to libraries over
e telephone without a distributor.

  —Yes, Dwayne said.

  —Isn't that the hard way?

  —No. The hard way is sending my work to jaded agents
d publishers and getting nowhere because they won't even read
y work. The hard way is waiting to be validated by that loop, by
at fraternal bunch of idiots who keep feeding us the same
ipe...by publishing the same stable of writers over and over
ecause of some commercial formula that makes money. No, the
ard way is waiting for them to open a door for me while I give up
y life and dreams to some dead-end job I hate. This way, at least,
m getting some readers. I actually enjoy going around those
nuckleheads. I know many writers who get published and are
iven a measly 3, 4 or 5% of the retail price, if they're lucky. Even
gents get at least 10%. I could go on and on about marketing
our own work, giving you a hot bath in self promotion. But that
oesn't work. You have to have the drive and risk yourself,
orrow money, do whatever it takes to put your writing out there.
ou must go beyond rejection and fear of failure.
ooking at Alissa, he said:

  —In fact I believe that because most writers are unwilling
 risk it all, that's why I prosper. If it was easy everybody would
e doing it. It's not easy.

e saw Alissa smile at him, then she listened to a comment from
e woman seated next to her.

  —Oh, before I forget, my sister Karen is a librarian in
rizona. She finds libraries where my books circulate. And she

schedules these book signings for me. I promised her I'd mention a fact about public libraries.

Dwayne reads from a bookmarker his sister sent him:

—Americans spend nine times as much on home video games—$1.5 billion—as they do on school library materials for their children. Wait, this one really scares me: In twenty-five years, federal funding for libraries comes to less than the cost of one aircraft carrier.

Another question:

—What do your initials D. H. stand for?

—Dwayne Harvey. Now you know why I use my initials.

—What's the plot of your new book?

—The plot. There is no plot. It's the first book in a series that will end when the leading character dies. See, I don't like to talk about my books I've written...or the one I'm working on. Mainly because it's something I've never been able to do. At least to my satisfaction. It's like a preview for a movie. It gives you this peek at the story. I don't like to say anything about my stories. I'm embarrassed by them when I talk about them. For me, it's like talking about a game or a relationship I was in and what I did in this game. Maybe I'm jaded from selling them and, perhaps, they are just tripe, not worthy of anyone's time. But I want you to know that your stories are the important ones—how you live your lives and how you tell your stories to the world is what's really important. Who cares about anyone's books? They're only long movies or stories to get lost in. I don't want my readers to know where they are going in my novels. I want them lost in the story. I'm here to, hopefully, sell some books.

—I want a copy of your new book, Alisa smiled from the back of the room.

—Great.

Dwayne went back to Alissa with a copy of his new book and stood before her:

—What's your first name? he smiled.

She smiled and spelled her name for him. After he signed the book, he handed it to her:

—How much is it? she asked.

—Ten bucks, he said.

When she paid him he asked:

—How are you?

—Fine.

Then: the black woman next to her said to Dwayne:

—Mr. Dayne, I want to get a copy for my grandchild.

As the elderly woman looked for money in her purse he went back to the front and got the woman a copy of his new book. He, again, saw how great Alissa's body looked in tight jeans when she stood near her chair.

—Who do you want me to sign it to? he asked the woman, hoping Alissa didn't leave just now.

—Jerilyn.

After she spelled her granddaughter's name, she handed him a business card with a Fredericksburg address and phone number printed on it. The rest of the card caught him off guard: The Wilderness / free first Tarot reading / by Ellouise.

Ellouise paid Dwayne from a huge wad of bills wound tight with crossed purple and yellow rubber bands. She told Dwayne to come by her place at two tomorrow afternoon. All he could do was nod yes and think of his brother telling him to go to The Wilderness.

He came back to his senses when he saw Ellouise waddle away, exiting the room. He turned to the sweet fragrance of Alissa. She looked ready to leave. He asked her to stay a bit and they left the library together after he sold five more books.

They walked together toward Sammy's where they first met. He had pointed to Traveller when they reached the front library sidewalk and told her that was his new home. She said:

—You always lived interesting.

He loved that trace of a lisp she still had; it was so adorable.

It was the same Alissa. She talked about her failed marriage to a womanizer she meet in Baltimore, a hockey player. No children. It wasn't until they reached Sammy's he could ask her where she was living now, and how she heard about his book signing. She said she was staying at her dad's house in Spotsylvania, and that she saw a flyer about his signing at the library. She said that she'd go to the library to research her next career move in real estate; and then she went on and on about her messy divorce for a half hour in Sammy's.

There was no laughter between them as before. Old flames seem to never be the same, he thought, while listening to the endless list of grievances against her ex-husband: he snored, he stayed out all night with his friends; he drank too much; he never took her out; and on and on.

Not once did she mention his writing, so he never mentioned Josie in *The Paper Man*.

Later: as they neared Traveller, he asked her where she parked, not wanting her company, for he was tired and wanted to get some sleep. She seemed disappointed, and gave him a look of rejection he had felt before with her when he hugged her goodbye so many years ago.

—Will you be in town for long? she asked.

—No...I'll call my sister tomorrow and find out where my next book signing is...and be off.

He watched her drive away in her Volvo; he sighed a big relief to have her problems gone. Just then, obscured by Traveller, was Ann's parked blue Escort; he could see her clothes piled on the back seat. He went over to her driver's-side door and saw her asleep on the front seat. He knocked lightly on her window. She smiled after jerking awake, happy to see him. Now he was really glad he hadn't invited Alissa in Traveller. When she rolled down window:

—What are you doin' here? he smiled.

—I missed your book signing, she pouted. How did it go?

—Great...sold a few books.

—I read your new book. I liked it.

ayne opened her door after she unlocked it; he took her hand
d helped her out of her car. Then, he kissed her. She responded
orably.

—I could use a shower, she laughed.

In Traveller, he lay in his boxers on top of his bed in the
ck bedroom listening to her shower water. He wanted to know
at happened to her at Appomattox, but that was not important
w. Soon, she may come into his bedroom.

She did. Covered breast high by a large bath towel, he
uld see her beautiful brown thighs standing in the narrow
orway. He moved over and patted the warm bottom flannel
eet where he was lying. She lay beside him on her back with one
ee raised, and holding the towel in place over her breasts.

They stared up at Traveller's ceiling as they had in Ben's
om at Dixieland. They remained quiet, breathing together. She
as happy to be here and did not feel like explaining her vanishing
t at Appomattox just now. He took hold of her right hand that
t so silky from lotion she had just put on. Her body smelled of
eet strawberries as he kept breathing deeply, taking in her sweet
grance. He covered them with a cool navy-blue comforter from
e foot of his bed and turned onto his left side to her, resting his
ht hand on her warm belly where the towel was creased open a
t. Her left hand covered the back of his fingers, touching and
essing them lightly as if she wanted him. Then, she released the
wel at her chest and moved his hand from her belly to her hard
easts.

But soon: waves of guilt swept over his lucky hand; he

lifted his hand from her breast and touched her cheek, turning her eyes into his, saying softly:

—I want to. But I see you as that abandoned baby.

—You paid it back...with interest, she smiled.

—I've got no business being with a girl half my age. A few years ago...I wouldn't think about it. But now it's different, Ann. He thought about saying: But don't listen to me.

She smiled that she understood and kissed his forehead. He squeezed her shoulder and turned her back to him, his arm over the comforter, he whispered:

—I must be gettin' old.

She laughed.

Then, he reached back onto his headboard shelf and grabbed the vile of joy she gave him. He unscrewed the cap and placed the vile near her nostrils. She inhaled the fragrance deeply, then, he did the same.

As he slept beside Ann in Traveller, a dream came fast:

The dream began with music playing. During a spin backwards the Boz Scaggs song *Sierra* played as Dwayne was back at Appomattox at the close of The Civil War. When he came out of his spin, the music stopped; Dwayne was about fourteen years old.

The boy Dwayne put on his glasses after squinting in yellow haze and dust. He could see he was wearing wool pants and cotton shirt and he was barefoot. He looked at his young body, touching his slender arms and legs before touching his young face.

On his feet he could hear dejected Confederate soldiers bemoaning Lee's surrender. Then, behind him, he heard a familiar voice from his past. It was Johnny's hoarse high-pitched tone calling:

—Dwayne!

There on the McClean front porch was his six-year-old brother Johnny with his bare white pot belly, bulbous bald head and bird

s, a sight for sore eyes, dressed in ragged wool pants and
efoot.

Young brothers now had all the memories of their forty
rs together. They were the ages of their turbulent childhood in
trailer. Dwayne tried out his voice to see if he could speak as
walked toward the porch:

—Johnny, is that you?

—Yeah, Johnny answered.

Their memories began to swim in their blue eyes. The lump
Dwayne's throat grew as they were able to see the same memory
gether. They saw:

they were sleeping in the same bed, in the trailer. Johnny
d wet the bed as he did nearly every night. Usually, Dwayne
uld wake up angry and punch his brother's thigh, giving him a
arlie horse for soaking their mattress.

But now: they see it the way Dwayne wished he had acted;
s was Dwayne's way of asking his brother for forgiveness. They
n see Dwayne waking up in the middle of the night on their pee-
t mattress. This time: Dwayne gently covers Johnny with dry
dding after removing his sleeping brother's wet underwear and
tting on a clean pair and removing the wet bottom sheet.

ck at Appomattox:

—I love you, Dwayne told his brother.

—I know. I love you, too.

Lee and Grant, two brothers, they embrace on the porch and
ter the McClean House to surrender all things from their past, a
ad past where all things are forgiven.

That night, with Ann in Traveller, was incredible. Though
sex, it meant more to Dwayne than a thousand nights with
ssa's perfect body. Or, at least ten nights, he mused, the

morning he awoke with Ann under his arm in the Fredericksburg parking lot.

He watched Ann get out of bed gracefully, and listened to her making coffee in his new home. He wanted to lie there alone and remember the dream he had before he said anything to Ann about it. Somewhere in his writing, he knew he would always mak his dreams an integral part of his characters, for he knew too well that dreams function to solve problems in waking life and to quicken the dreamer's new potentials.

Regarding Alissa, he made a mental note to write about returning to an old flame after years of separation. Everything had changed between them. And there seems to be some immutable law about time that says you can't go home again. Even the thought of being with that perfect body had waned. It was, by far, his rudest awakening for getting older. Not once in his life had he thought about turning away a beautiful woman, or any woman, wh wanted to be with him...until last night.

Even the faintest hint about love was not there, for Alissa o Ann, two beautiful women who had been on his mind many times. What is this, he wondered, this inability to take her, something he had always been able to do without hesitation? And is this the way it will be for me from now on? Or does it even get worse from here, for God's sake? Is this why old men look old, worn out, unable to bring lead to their pencils? If so: why hasn't modern medicine done something about it by now? Why have they not found a way to make the mind stay young? Will I be wandering North America like some flaccid moron with a dead pencil?

He sat at Traveller's cozy booth in his boxers and T-shirt watching Ann pour their coffee. Her cheerful "Good morning" an smile—he wanted every morning. He said:

—You are shifting my life...in a good way...aren't you?
Her face showed nothing she was hiding from him as she sat across from him blowing on her hot coffee. Then a big smile:

—Why do you say that?

—Last night I dreamed of being with my brother. It was so real. And Appomattox...that was unreal. If you are that same girl who was abandoned, and now you have your money, why are you still here and why am I seeing these things since you came into my life?

They watched each other sip their coffee. She said:

—It was you who came into my life, Dwayne...many years ago...remember? I thought about how you created a character in *White Shoulders* who was abandoned and then you found me. When you stabbed your pen into Thomas Wolfe's grave, you told me you made a pledge to live your life to your full potential. When you paid back your pledge to me, it opened you up and freed you to see your brother. All kinds of people will come into your life now that you're open to it. Just make sure they're good for you.

—So...you're not some angel or force that brings me these things I see?

—I'm just a woman, with a new friend.

She put her hand out to him on the tabletop and he held it gently. He said:

—I want you to stay with me for a while, if you can.

—I really can't stay long.

—What do you have to get back to?

—My life, she smiled.

He nodded, understanding, then added:

—Ya know, one of the last things my brother told me when I turned him down when he wanted to sell my books was "I guess I'm being selfish."

—You've got some healing to do, Dwayne. Your brother meant a lot to you, I know. Stay open to seeing things and you'll get stronger.

—That dream I had last night about him—I thought you were the reason I could see such a thing. I'm not sure I could live alone and see those things. Ya know what I mean?

She nodded yes, and he continued:

—In the dream, I stared at my brother's sparkling blue eyes. They were so clear and healthy and had this liquid glow of light in them that was far from his bi-polar glaze before he died. Then, I looked deeper into his eyes, but they were my eyes. Or, rather, the healthy eyes of my full potential.

The realization that Ann could not help him see his life or quicken his potential of what he can become—it had to be all his or nothing. There was no use in asking her why his salubrious eyes in his dream were his brother's eyes. Ann could only reflect what he was willing to see. And that's why he didn't want her to leave, for he liked having a woman around who could just let him be without judgment, without wanting to change him. That American trap of being happy or complete when the right one comes along, just had to be dropped, or he'd never live in the present or develop as a writer, a lover, a man. As they drank their coffee:

—Ann, I want you to do what makes you happy. When you're with me, I'll enjoy it. And when you go, I'll be happy for you.

God, I wish I'd begged her to stay, he scolded himself while hiking alone to the top of Mayre's Hill in Fredericksburg. He was wearing denim jeans and jacket with a clean gray flannel shirt and brown walking shoes. His face is clearly stubbled with gray, and if not for his blue eyes he would be a dead ringer for the younger Captain R. E. Lee.

Ann left in her car after she showered, heading back home to Oregon to go to school. When they hugged goodbye outside her car, she whispered to him:

—Thank you for making the world new again. I had to find you and tell you that.

He knew what she meant. And it never entered his mind to grill her why she left him at Appomattox, until now, as he approached the exact spot where Uncle Robert stood watching his infantry slaughter wave after wave of Yankees who stormed uphill, out from behind the stone wall into a maelstrom of Rebel lead.

Dwayne imagined and could hear deafening artillery fire and battle sounds while looking through the thumb ends of his scanning and fisted hands as if binoculars. He surveyed down to a distant stone wall where Union soldiers were mowed down during the Battle of Fredericksburg. The imagined sounds of wounded and dying men are horrific until he moved his makeshift binoculars to the serene downtown business district of Fredericksburg, where he sees quaint church steeples that are partly obscured in a purplish pink October mist of quick rain and sunshine.

Then, below him, his fisted binoculars let him see the Sunken Road before the Confederate stone wall where Lee's troops fired their lead storm into the blue. Behind Dwayne is a historical marker with a quote from the commander on this spot during the Battle of Fredericksburg: "It is well that war is so terrible, else we would grow too fond of it."

To himself, after putting down his hands, Dwayne mumbled:
—It is good that self-publishing is so terrible...else everyone would do it.

From inside his denim jacket he slid out his black leather notebook Blacky, and balanced on one knee while writing upon it: Always when I stand on Mayre's Hill I feel connected to him, full of hope and energy. I said goodbye to an angel this morning who could've been Lee's beloved Annie in another life. Am I related to them? I do not know. As D. H. Lawrence said, "Facts are quite unimportant, only 'truths' matter." I truly believe I'm related to him. That's all that matters to me.

The address on the business card Ellouise gave him was near Dwayne's old apartment near the river. Lawn Boy was with him in the empty parking lot at the bottom of Mayre's Hill.

Chris Rea's song *I Can Hear Your Heartbeat* played from Lawn Boy's cassette player all the way to The Wilderness, the ominous name of Ellouise's Tarot reading business and the name his brother said to go to at Appomattox.

During the song, Dwayne's heart pumped vexation; he kept thinking of Ann driving all the way across the country in her little car with all that cash on her. Not until he realized he was into the unrealness of what he wanted, only then did he tell himself to "STOP IT," and then he imagined Ann driving safely home without trouble.

Ellouise had no signage advertising her business outside her home, only a gold-painted mailbox with a rainbow of incursive letters that spelled The Wilderness. Her porch was dark and the windows draped shut. On the porch were dozens of empty clay pots for plants that were arranged orderly on antique chairs and tables and unfinished shelves; and along the floor many of the pots were conjoined to cobwebs in a thousand places. To himself he quipped:

—If she's got a black cat, I'm outta here.

Ellouise answered her door, smiling, liking this polite man right off for being punctual. Her parlor was organized chaos, yet despite its clutter had form and purpose with sunny colors of sherbets and a massive bright raspberry oval rug under dark solid-wood furniture. Before she sat:

—Can I get you some tea or coffee?

–No, thanks. I've been anxious to know about this reading You said you talked to my sister.

When 74-year-old Ellouise Haynes laughed, her wide frame jiggled like brown Jell-o as she waddled and wedged herself into her favorite chair across from Dwayne.

—Yes..ah, Lord mercy...your sister Karen is one funny, funny girl. You know what I mean.

He couldn't help but notice that the old lady had a large mole that covered the inside of her left ear; it had a cluster of black hairs like grasshopper antennae growing out of it.

—Your sister e-mailed me because I'm a member of the Virginia Genealogical Society, specializing in past life regression therapy. She gave me information on your lineage, your bloodline...and I just had to get you in touch with my granddaughter Jerilyn. My Jerilyn, she is the sweetest girl, and talented. Lord, she's been given it all, that girl.

Dwayne cleared his throat stopping himself from asking what this has to do with him. Then, he saw Jerilyn's picture on an end table:

—Is that her?

—Yes, that's my Jerilyn.

—She's a knockout, he smiled.

On a coffee table between them, Ellouise removed a silk scarf from a deck of eleven "Tree of Life" Tarot Cards that had already been turned up and read. She turned on a small lamp that lit up the faces of each card.

—I read this yesterday with your sister.

—On the computer?

—Yes.

—Is this reading mine or my sister's?

—A little bit of both. Your relationship to Mr. Lee is what made me think you can help my Jerilyn.

—Help her? Wait...did you find out for sure I'm related to Robert E. Lee? Wait! Don't tell me. But what does this have to do with me helping your granddaughter?

—She has a boyfriend who keeps her stuck.

—Stuck?

—I believe he has a past life trauma that traps them in his pain. You and Jerilyn together can free the three of you.

—Why me?

He followed her eyes down to one of the eleven colorful cards shining under the green light bulb.

—Did my sister tell you I may be related to Lee?

—Yes.

—Could you find out for sure if I'm related to him?

—Yes, it would take me a few days.

—No, no. I don't want to know—not now, anyway. But how can I help your granddaughter if helping her means I have to be related to Lee?

Ellouise laughed, having a good time with this writer, saying:

—You don't have to be related. You only have to believe you are. Belief is hope. Hope is life, Mr. Dayne. Tree of Life will show the path of "the Lightning Flash."

—Lightning Flash?

—The thought of God manifesting in the physical world.

When she pointed to a Tarot Card on the table, its cosmic design strange to Dwayne:

—Isn't this some kind of occult thing?

Ellouise laughed so hard she flatulated; she leaned back in her chair patting her chubby hands together, lightly touching her fingertips.

—Can't ya be hypnotized and find out about past life stuff?

—No. My Jerilyn's boyfriend has a debilitating past life contract.

—Contract?

—Trauma from a past life where the person was the perpetrator. Or, it could be holding onto being victimized by a perpetrator. Nasty stuff, Mr. Dayne...and you gotta big connection to my Jerilyn somehow.

—Why me?

He followed her eyes, again down to one of the eleven cards on the table between them. She hesitated to feel the card he was looking at just at that moment. She said:

—I asked your sister to write out a question she wants answered. I wrote it down on the back of this card. She said it would be your question, too.

She had given the card to Dwayne a few seconds ago. He flipped the card over and peeled off a self-adhesive note and read it out loud:

—Is my brother Johnny in a better place?

The next morning: Dwayne was nearing Richmond in Traveller with Lawn Boy in tow. Ellouise had given him an admission ticket that was used as a book marker in her bible. Ellouise told Dwayne that she would call Jerilyn and let her know that she gave him her ticket and the book he signed for her in the library. The old lady told him that Jerilyn would be open to meeting him and helping him answer his and Karen's question about their brother. He had watched Ellouise put on her reading glasses and squint at the date printed on the ticket. She was not sure of the date and asked him if it was tomorrow night. He read what he could see in her dark parlor:

—Ms. Virginia..yes..tomorrow at 8 PM at Richmond Auditorium.

As he took an exit to get gas and directions to the Richmond Auditorium, he thought of Jerilyn, so beautiful and talented, and how every Sunday she sings at her father's Gospel Church near Lee's monument.

Downtown Richmond: the Confederate Museum has one of the finest Civil War collections. Jerilyn Lee Haynes, 31-year-old tour guide, is speaking to a group of adults near an encased uniform of Robert E. Lee. Her black hair is pinned up; she's wearing a conservative gray business suit with low heels. She's using her Southern accent for the benefit of the tour. Her soft voice echoes in the drafty museum:

—This is General Lee's uniform worn during most of his battles. If you look closely at his boots you'll see...

-175-

A bigot's voice interrupted:

—Marse Robert's boots need a Nigger shine!

Jerilyn's eyes widen like liquid almonds, her dark skin concealing her blush. She gave the obese white bigot a stern look. The man was chewing gum with this big insolent grin on his ruddy face, a face that looked like a toad with red welts all over his cheeks and gouty neck. But Jerilyn remained cool, ignoring the bigot as her group became more uneasy. Then, coming from behind her group she sees the worst thing possible; she prays fast that there's not a scene.

A well-dressed black man, 45, strong, tall, intense, short-tempered; his eyes are now like dry black grapes—ready to squeeze the life out of something or somebody. His name is William Howard Ellison. He winks at Jerilyn while he stands behind the bigot unnoticed by all except Jerilyn, his girlfriend and client. William's from Baltimore, visiting Jerilyn for the pageant tonight; he also has a Masters Degree in American History.

Jerilyn, not wanting any trouble, nearly skips Lee's boots but continues:

—The General's boots...

—Need a Nigger shine! the redneck barked.

Jerilyn was naturally sweet and shy; she remained calm as William's jaw tightened with anger. She gave her boyfriend a look that told him to let her handle this, please.

—Sir, I'll have to ask you to leave the building if you persist with such outbursts, Jerilyn said.

—Yer pretty uppity for a Nigger girl!

The bigot's surprised from behind by a polished Northern accent:

—I believe the lady made an error.

William stood close to the man; they face each other as the group disperses, as William continued:

—Her error was calling you sir. Because only an ignorant bastard like yourself wouldn't know that Marse Robert was a true

ntleman, willing to shine any man's boots, just for the good of it.
he General would also be quick to order your impish mouth shut
d out of his sight.

he bigot's startled by William's intense demeanor and intelligence
hen he adds in a Southern accent:

  —Or would you prefer I Nigger shine yer empty head?

he bigot fearfully exited the museum. With her group gone,
illiam walked over to Jerilyn and said with a smile that he did well
t to wail on that idiot. She replied:

  —I know.

e watched his girlfriend of two years walk away; he followed her
rough a door that led out to the museum balcony that overlooked
e James River and the city of Petersburg.

  Jerilyn faced the view while William looked at her profile
d said:

  —You're anxious about the pageant.

e was confused; her eyes stayed across the river to the dark
icks of Petersburg when she said:

  —This Ms. Virginia thing...I don't know...it's a product...a
rfume...an image.

illiam bent down close to her neck and smelled the sweet
agrance she started to wear upon her decision to enter the Ms.
rginia pageant competition, and he whispered in a mocking
uthern drawl:

  —Shore smells good on yew, Miz Virginia.

ey laugh then kiss. Their faces close after kissing, he whispered:

  —I'm your business manager, correct?

e smiled, nodding yes.

  —This is a business decision. You are Ms. Virginia.

e looked away; he gently turned her beautiful face back to his
d said softly:

  —Baby...this is everything we've worked for. The
deling, voice lessons, the practice, the wardrobe. A couple of

years of being Ms. Virginia and we're living our dream. You are Ms. Virginia.

They embraced. But she cannot see that William's eyes are pained when looking at Petersburg across the river; he suddenly gets a sharp wincing pain in his left arm that he conceals from Jerilyn. He closed his eyes and held her close to him.

Dwayne left his vehicles parked in the Richmond Auditorium parking lot in the very back in the last row. The six long city blocks to the Richmond downtown business district area was a pleasant walk in 60 degrees of clear sky and no wind. In the Yellow Pages he found his old Fredericksburg chiropractor who moved his practice to Richmond. Dr. Blythe specialized in neuro-emotional technique without manual adjusting, something his body preferred.

If he had time, Dwayne wanted to go see Jerilyn at the Confederate Museum, give her his book and discuss past lives. He also wanted to see Libby Prison nearby the James River, a famous prison where a distant relative on his father's side was incarcerated and from which he had escaped. But first: he wanted a session with Dr. Blythe.

It was always strange after a session with the doctor how strangers were so friendly and receptive to him. And with October slipping away, Dwayne knew that cold weather would drive him into those aches and pains only a self-published writer knows if he didn't get adjusted soon.

Step after step he felt the joy of being here in the moment in Richmond in October on these Richmond streets so clean and prosperous and loaded with history. Pride had more than a distinct presence on passing faces and in the sounds around him in every little thing his pale blue eyes saw as his feet tread softly on downtown Richmond sidewalks lined with young elms, yellow birc and sycamores.

Yes, this was the true heart and soul of the rebellion, a
fiance that yet remains on the faces of natives, faces that would
y if they could—they'd like to try it again. Without Richmond:
th sides would have lost half the men they did. All that carnage
save this city of seven hills; to preserve this Southern pride; and
maintain a way of life that Southern men were prepared to die
r, much more so than a Northern man.

Richmond women were sustaining this pride even today.
hey reminded him of Michigan women with their strikingly
autiful hardiness. It was there in their posture and tight jawline;
ings that revealed a strength and leanness that can endure severe
rdships amidst chaos and rigid conditions; and yet remain refined
d poised above it all. It had to be in their genes. When in the
mpany of such women, men will do anything for them—even go
war.

Before long: he was at Dr. Blythe's office. The October
n shone brightly on his bronze nameplate outside his office front
or. Lucky for Dwayne: he was able to get worked right in
ithout an appointment.

After patient and doctor exchanged polite conversation, the
xty-year-old chiropractor ushered his old patient into an
amination room. With Dwayne on his back, on a treatment table,
e doctor tested him with a series of tests involving his feet and
rtical arm strength resistance at each wrist that determined what
d where he was holding onto negative emotions.

—My wife read your first book. She really enjoyed the
ory.
uring more finger-tapping on several places:

—Great.
he doctor tapped and pressed his fingertips on Dwayne's forehead
d told his patient to think about his main complaint. Right away,
hat came to mind was "selfish." As Dr. Blythe tested the writer's
sistance by holding Dwayne's wrist as Dwayne's arm is raised

vertically:

—Resist. Eyes closed...resist. Now, looking down with your eyes closed, think of your main complaint and the number 1. Quickly, the doctor moved down to Dwayne's feet, spreading them apart, then together a few times.

—Okay, on your stomach. What's the title of that book?

—*Ledges*.

—Yes.

Blythe felt for subluxations along Dwayne's spine, going back and forth to his feet, checking leg length:

—Think of your number one complaint. Again...but hold your breath with your eyes closed while thinking about your complaint.

When Dwayne was told to get up, he handed the doctor a piece of paper he kept in his pocket.

—Will you test me on this?

He looked at the question on the piece of paper and Dwayne extended his left arm while the doctor tested resistance to:

—Is your brother in a better place?

His arm dropped easily, then Blythe tapped his patient's chest and again tested resistance. This time it held strong. The doctor asked him if this emotion is inherited by his parents. His arm held strong, indicating no. Then:

—Second generation?

Still holds.

—Third?

Still holds.

—Fourth?

No change.

—Fifth?

Dwayne's arm drops easily, indicating:

—You inherited this painful emotion five generations ago.

The doctor looks at Dwayne's piece of paper and tests whether this painful emotion happened during a Civil War battle. His arm fell, indicating yes.

From list:

  —Was it Fredericksburg?

No.

  —Chancellorville?

He still holds. Again to the list on the paper:

  —Gettysburg?

Still strong; same with The Wilderness. Then:

  —Petersburg?

His arm drops easily; his arm hurts and he's tired.

  —You inherited this emotion five generations ago during the Battle of Petersburg.

  —Couldn't my body subconsciously want to believe this happened so long ago that I'm not responsible?

  —Your body doesn't lie.

  —This is so strange because I'm related to Robert E. Lee on my mother's side...married into the Lee Family after the war. For years I thought I had inherited his pain genetically. But it's not that at all, or I would have tested weak at all those battles.

The doctor nodded in agreement and wonder.

  Jerilyn and William had just finished lunch; they're chatting when their waiter returned with William's credit card and bad news:

  —I'm sorry, Mr. Ellison, your charge on your card was declined.

William's embarrassed.

  —There must be some mistake.

  —I ran it through twice, sir.

As William searched his pockets for cash, Jerilyn handed the waiter her credit card. The waiter left with Jerilyn's card as William counted his cash, hoping he had enough on him.

  —My treat, William.

He handed his girlfriend his money saying that lunch was his treat.

—And paying for it is mine, she smiled.

William smiled and swallowed his pride, stuffing his cash back into his pocket before he proposed a toast with his wine glass:

—To Ms. Virginia.

Jerilyn toasted with her water glass as:

Ellouise Haynes removed a jeweler's ring case from a hiding place and opened it. She picked out a man's gold wedding band and stared at the ring in the palm of her hand. Then she clenched her hand and held it against her heart.

William winced from pain in his left arm after parking his car in front of Jerilyn's apartment in Richmond.

—William, what's wrong, baby?

—I'm fine. Lately I've had this pain in my arm. It goes away. I'm fine. Prob'ly an old football injury.

He leaned over and kissed Jerilyn, adding:

—Course I'd feel a lot better if I could rest a bit in your apartment.

—Not now. Tonight's a big night.

—I know. Can't blame me for tryin'.

—Where are you staying? she asked.

—I've got a reservation at the Ramada. It's a real nice hotel. I'll see ya tonight, Ms. Virginia.

She smiled and kissed him quick before hustling into her brownstone. William watched her until the front door closed behind her, then he drove away.

Jerilyn entered her nicely furnished one-bedroom apartment after unlocking the door. She sorted through her mail, then stopped to play her messages on her answering machine:

—Hey, Jerilyn! It's yer ole granny wishin' you well tonight. I can't be there. My tired feet won't take me to Richmond. I gave

ny ticket to a writer named Dwayne. He's a nice man. You can
alk to this man about your dreams and past lives. Have fun! Love
va. And God bless.
'erilyn smiled, put down her mail and walked outside to her cubed
>atio balcony. She looked south across the river toward Petersburg
s:

Dwayne's walking the cobblestone back streets around
_ibby Prison along the riverfront in Richmond's historical district.
He was thinking:
—I know I was here during that war. I can feel it: the
onely hours and months and months of waiting and holding on with
ittle food or decent clothing. I've always managed to avoid going
o the crater in Petersburg...and Dr. Blythe's session proved it. It's
so true: face what you fear and grow. If you don't, you walk this
earth on coward's legs, shaky and ready to run from fear to fear.
With his back to the red brick walls of the two-century old
_ibby Prison, facing the river, he could see the hills and
smokestacks of Petersburg to the south. Maybe that would lead
aim out of his Wilderness, a path leading to one day when he can
ruly love again and get out of this restlessness that keeps him from
>eing a writer/in, the slash being the door that Thomas Wolfe wrote
about.
It was but a few hours until Ms. Virginia. He decided to get
_awn Boy and drive over to Petersburg.

William's car is parked outside his Motel 6 room. He's
dressed, lying on his back watching television. He's uncomfortable
and hot, so he turns on the A/C and walks over to the sink. When
ae turns on the light he gets a bigger shooting pain in his left arm
that keels him over to the bed when:

On the drive over to Petersburg, Dwayne's legs are weak

and his breathing labored as sweat pours off him. He parked Lawn Boy on Plank Road at the base of the Petersburg crater some six blocks away. He could not walk far, for he began to feel nauseous. He sat on the curb, and laid back trying to breathe deep with his eyes closed while stroking his upset stomach as:

William's writhing and moaning, screaming in agony on his motel bed as:

Jerilyn's taking a bath, crying about something.

That evening: William parked his car in front of Jerilyn's apartment building. He's wearing a business suit that's wrinkled some. He opens his back passenger door as Jerilyn came out carrying a large purse and clothing bag. After he put her things on the back seat, they drove away talking:
　—Did you get a nap in?, she asked.
　—Yeah.
　—How's your arm?
　—Just fine. You get some rest?
　—No. I kept thinking about tonight.
　—Nervous?
　—Remember those dreams I've been having?
　—The dreams of 1864?, he asked, half laughing.
She turned away angry, facing her window.
　—I'm sorry, baby. I promised not to make light of your dreams..and..I'm sorry. What about your dream?
She turned back to him:
　—This is no dream. I felt it during my bath. I was afraid..to see it again.
　—Tell me again about the part you don't want to see.
　—All of it. It's so real I can't even explain it.
　—Okay. After you win this competition..you girl.. are

aking a couple days off..with me.
he smiled as:

Dwayne's parked in Lawn Boy on Plank Road listening to
Chris Rea's *I Can Hear Your Heartbeat*.

Later: William's waiting patiently outside a dressing room
oor when Jerilyn came out modeling her gown for him. She
urned like a pro as William smiled his approval as other Ms.
Virginia contestants came in and out of the dressing room as:

Dwayne's writing up a storm behind Lawn Boy's wheel.
This is what he's written:
After seeing Dr. Blythe, I was convinced to come to Petersburg to
he crater. I could not make it to the crater because my breathing
became abnormal on Plank Road. I felt like I was having a heart
ttack so I returned to Lawn Boy. I believe there's something
elated to these chest pains and Uncle Robert's bad heart. I once
hought my angel from Asheville, Ann, might be Annie Lee, Lee's
daughter who died during the war. I was wrong about that. I need
o go to the crater, but I might die trying. I know not why I'm
writing this down. No clue. Perhaps it's leading me to a space
where I can let go of my brother. I know I did not do all that I
ould to even give him hope for living in this world. Perhaps I'm
oining him here in this place so far from any family or friends.
Karen knows why I'm here. She told Ellouise Haynes in
Fredericksburg about my connection to Uncle Robert. It led me
ere after seeing Dr. Blythe in Richmond. I'm off to see Ms.
Virginia at the Richmond Auditorium..God willing. D. H. Dayne.

Jerilyn and contestants chat in a back stage dressing room
while fixing their hair and putting on makeup:

—I heard Ms. Virginia will get all kinds of movie roles and full-page ads in *Vogue* and *Cosmopolitan*, the contestant with a Southern accent said as she picks up a bottle of the Ms. Virginia perfume and dabs a drop behind each ear.

The contestant displayed the bottle smiling:

—And for that kind of money..I don't care where they scratch and sniff.

Jerilyn and other contestants laugh.

Outside: the auditorium's jammed with parked cars for the pageant.

Inside: there's a full house as the pageant's about to begin. William sits on an aisle seat next to Jerilyn's parents, Reverend Haynes, a middle-aged black man and Mrs. Haynes, a middle-aged white woman. Granny Haynes' empty seat is next to Mr. Haynes. All are dressed formally.

As the house lights go down, an usher points at Dwayne's seat for him. Dwayne's wearing a sports jacket with clean jeans as he approaches his seat. The pageant announcer's voice:

—Welcome, ladies and gentlemen, to the Ms. Virginia Pageant! Let's give a big Richmond welcome to your host tonight..Bob Baker!

During the applause, William's arm starts to bother him as Dwayne nears his seat. Right when William and the stranger make eye contact: they both vomit at the same time. The Haynes couple and nearby audience members are shocked and repulsed as William pulls his hanky and covers his mouth while hurrying up the aisle after Dwayne. Dry heaving, they hunt and scurry for a restroom. Dwayne followed William into the restroom.

William's barfing into the john in his open-door stall as Dwayne does the same in the adjacent stall. They exit the stalls at the same time to clean up at the sink area; they look exhausted. William, looking into the mirror while cleaning up:

—Man, I've never done that before.

—Me neither.

William uses some breath spray. Dwayne points to the breath spray:

—May I?

—Sure.

After wiping off their jackets, they exit the restroom together.

Dwayne sits next to Mr. Haynes, to William's surprise, as the pageant continues with contestants modeling in sleek fashion dresses on the runway near them. William's curious why this stranger is sitting next to Mr. Haynes and himself.

It's Jerilyn's turn to walk down the runway. The pageant host tells the audience:

—Our next contestant is from Richmond...Jerilyn Ann Haynes!

The audience applauds. As William and Jerilyn's parents applaud, Dwayne is awestruck upon seeing Jerilyn. Jerilyn smiles down at William and her parents, then, she is visibly shaken to a diminished smile when she first lays eyes on Dwayne. She recovers her composure as the next contestant follows her down the runway.

William's left arm is bothering him as Dwayne's eyes follow Jerilyn until she's backstage and out of his view. Jerilyn's peeking at Dwayne discreetly from behind a curtain as other contestants are coming and going. Jerilyn walked away after a contestant asked her what she was looking at.

When Jerilyn and contestants are changing clothes, Jerilyn sees something flash as if from a past life: She's in a Richmond basement in 1864 at night. She is dressed like a servant slave; her name is Shy Ann, early 20's, and she's removing her blood-stained clothing, nervously soaking and scrubbing them in a large wooden tub by candlelight.

She comes out of her flashback looking scared; her hands are trembling as she zips up the back on her black, silk dress, then hustles out of the dressing room to wait nervously in the wings until

-187-

she's called out by the host for the talent competition.

When Jerilyn walks out to the microphone and nods to the band that's she's ready, she's stunned by what only she sees in the audience:

From Shy Ann's POV, she sees hundreds of frenzied torch-bearing Richmond residents preparing for war and waving Confederate flags.

William and her parents are surprised that she faltered and missed her cue to sing when the band began playing The Marvelettes' song *When The Hunter Gets Captured By The Game*. Dwayne also sees what Jerilyn sees in 1861 Richmond.

He is in his Richmond home in 1861; his name is now Lieutenant Jeb Clayton, 35; he's modeling his new Confederate uniform for his wife Mary and young servant Shy Ann. All are happy and alive as war nears. End of flashback.

Dwayne's perspiring heavily in his seat; he's focused intensely on Jerilyn as she finishes singing with her eyes closed. When she finishes the song, she opens her eyes to robust applause. William can see Jerilyn and the stranger next to him making eye contact, and how it appears to affect her.

Later: Jerilyn is announced as the new Ms. Virginia and winner of one hundred thousand dollars. But Dwayne is leaving the auditorium.

In Traveller: Dwayne is calling his sister on his cell phone. Karen asked if he met Ellouise.

—Yes! And I just left this pageant in Richmond and saw a crowd of people from the Civil War era! No kidding!

—I believe you.

—Ellouise's granddaughter was one of the contestants...and only we could see these people, I know!

—Jerilyn?

—Yes! What's goin' on, Karen?

—Dwayne, you have to be real careful now. You and

Jerilyn share this strong past life connection.

—Are you sure? How do you know? You sit there in front of your computer and read all these things but you're not really experiencing it! This is real, Karen!

—I know. I know. You don't have to be in Richmond and see where this goes, Dwayne. I can find a library nearby that'll want you for a signing. You're the one who wanted to change your life and do this. You're right. I sit here and play with these charts, and...I don't want you to get involved with something dangerous that I can't do.

—Yeah, he sighed. Ellouise said that you and I both wanted to know if Johnny's in a better place. I can't help but think that this will help me find that out.

—Well...I already know he's with Jesus. And that is a better place. I told Ellouise that was my question...because I know how much you want to believe it.

—Yeah. How can you mix Jesus with past lives? Isn't the Bible all or nothing?

—I have my faith. There's only one Savior no matter how many times you've been in this world. It's all good, Dwayne. Jesus will protect you.

—You know I don't like to be preached to. I'm an agnostic...and preachin' turns me off.

—It's all good, Dwayne.

—I know. It's all good. Ya know that Ann from Asheville?

—Yeah.

—She went back home to Oregon. I paid her the money I owed her from *White Shoulders*...with interest.

—That's a load off, huh?

—Yeah. I really liked her. She's too young for me...but I really liked her.

—Don't be boinkin' Baby Jane, Dwayne. And Jerilyn has a

boyfriend.

—I know. He's a pretty big guy, too. You have my next library lined up?

—I'm workin' on it.

—I gotta know soon, Karen.

—I know. Hey...a quarter of all U. S. schools have no school librarian.

Dwayne has Lawn Boy parked next to Traveller on the auditorium parking lot. The way he felt in Petersburg was a sign that something big was going to happen. After talking with Karen he wrote for a while, catching up with his experiences in Fredericksburg, Petersburg, and here in Richmond at the pageant. But now, he was this frustrated writer who could not get to the heart of any good writing. It was as if being here, after the things he saw in the auditorium, something was pushing him along other lines alien to writing, lines drawn by opposing armies, perhaps, he thought. She saw it, too, he knew. Again: Ms. Virginia saw it, too. He called Ellouise and found out where to find her tomorrow.

Next morning: Jerilyn's singing in her father's small church choir as Reverend Haynes sings along from his pulpit. Mrs. Haynes and William stand together in the front row singing from a hymn book. William's eyes see Jerilyn's eyes see someone enter the church at the back pew area. Dwayne's dressed casually as he stands with the congregation in the back row. William's confused and concerned about this stranger as he returns to his hymn book. Just then: William's face contorts in pain from his quivering left arm. The hymn ends.

Reverend Haynes motions for his congregation to be seated, then speaks from the pulpit:

—I thank you all for coming and sharing love and peace in the Lord's house. God bless.

The organist plays as the mostly black congregation files out.

In the church basement Dwayne pours himself a cup of coffee. He sees Jerilyn laughing and chatting with church members who are congratulating her for winning Ms. Virginia. Across the room William sees the stranger approach his beautiful girlfriend. She returns Dwayne's smile and is very shy around this man for some reason.

—I loved your singing...at the pageant...here, too.

—Thanks, she smiled with a nervous laugh that William could hear from across the room.

—I met your grandmother. She said you had some interesting dreams.

—You're the writer!

He handed her his book Ellouise bought for her. She looks it over, saying thank you several times and:

—I could write a book about these dreams I have.

—Can we go outside and talk?

—Sure.

When Jerilyn was leaving the basement with the stranger she motioned to her boyfriend that she'd be back soon. William waved back to her with a fake smile, then he watched them head upstairs.

They walked toward the Robert E. Lee monument a block away.

—Ever since I was a little girl, Granny Haynes has told me about her grandmother's life and experiences while she lived in Richmond during the Civil War. Back then my family could not read or write...so the stories passed on were our history.

They continued walking and talking until they reached the Lee monument whereupon lawn sprinklers came on. When Dwayne tried to warn her he called her Shy Ann. That's when she froze, both ignoring the sprinklers and getting sprayed:

—You called me Shy Ann.

Their eyes locked from some strange bond as if they shared past lives together, still getting sprayed by the sprinklers as Dwayne responds mesmerized:

   —At the pageant I felt I knew you. You felt it, too. We were here during those war years, Jerilyn. Do you get that?
She nods yes, then they move away from the sprinklers and cross the street to a small park. They stand close together on the grass:

   —You've been drawn to this Ms. Virginia stuff to resolve a past life, I think, to understand some lesson or something...I don't really know. All I know is there's something real going on here.

   —In my dreams there is a man...an officer from a family I worked for...in his house in Richmond. I think it was you. That's what threw me off last night when I saw you in the audience.

   —I can't say I've seen you in dreams...but I just know you are connected to my past life.
Dwayne grabs her shoulders:

   —Jerilyn, do you know me from a past life?
Their eyes and emotions are glowing with intensity as he's gripping her shoulders and squeezing them, pulling her to him:

   —I've been all over the South trying to find out who I was. I think I'm related to General Lee but I'm not sure. We have to resolve our pasts to be who we are. Something happened at Petersburg...
Jerilyn's startled by William's voice:

   —Jerilyn! You okay?
After Dwayne releases his hold on Jerilyn, they are awkward around William's bearing and protective posture.

   —William...this is Dwayne.

   —Dwayne Dayne. We met last night, Dwayne said.

   —Dwayne, William's my good friend and business manager.
William moved closer to Jerilyn with hard eyes for Dwayne. Dwayne changes the subject:

   —William, congratulations last night.
William nods coldly.

—William has a masters degree in history. Dwayne writes
novels.
William's not impressed when she hands him Dwayne's book:
     —Granny bought it for me. He even signed it to me.
Granny gave Dwayne her ticket to the pageant.
William nods, but Dwayne wants to leave:
     —Well, uh...I gotta go. Congratulations. Nice meeting ya
both.
William's fake smile and nod angers Jerilyn.
     —Bye, Dwayne.
Jerilyn gives her boyfriend a stern look as the writer walks away:
     —You weren't exactly friendly.
     —I don't like that guy. He irritates the hell outta me for
some reason.
     —You don't even know the man.
     —And you do?
     —I just met him. William, you are jealous.
     —I'm not jealous. I'm curious why you two were having
such an intense conversation for having just met.
     —Maybe we knew each other in a past life.
     —You're not serious?
She walks ahead of him, but William catches up:
     —So, this guy talks about your past lives together...and...all
your crazy dreams.
     —They're not crazy!
     —All I know is...you get a hundred grand and this...
stranger's into your dreams!
     —You are my manager! You damn sure don't run my
personal life!
Then, William mocks her:
     —Dwayne, this is my good friend. We've just made love
maybe a hundred times, talked about marriage and having kids...
nothing special.

—Fuck off, William!

William gets in front of her as Jerilyn shouts:

—You'll get your ten percent...then you can get in someone else's face!

He holds her arms while standing his ground:

—Baby, I'm sorry. Look, we just came off a big win...and I know I haven't been foolin' you with my one suit...stayin' in cheap motels with no credit cards. It's some big pride thing...I don't know. I'm creating first-generation wealth here. I'm breakin' through this poverty hell, baby.

She can see that his arm hurts as he lets them fall, and continues:

—You're the best thing I've ever known...and I have so many dreams for you that...all this other stuff just gets in the way. They walk, holding hands, into the church.

When Dwayne returned home he had a warning ticket to move Traveller off the lot. He forgot to get Jerilyn's phone number, not knowing if she even lived in Richmond. A woman like that would not have a listed number, he knew.

After loading Lawn Boy onto the trailer he drove back to her father's church, writing down the name of the church and her father's name from the church directory on the front lawn. With Blacky in hand, he walked back to Uncle Robert's monument; he stood before it, looking up at the 30-foot-high marble likeness of the general on Traveller. He sat on a nearby bench and began writing on paper from Blacky, describing the barren gray/lean trees standing at attention for the general. The middle-class homes were well maintained around him as if wanting to please the "gray fox." Yet, he noticed that there is an ignorance here, a natural integument obscuring the massive marble likeness of a man so important to us all. For he knew that this man on Traveller, if he had won at Gettysburg, may indeed have been the warrior who ended the war sooner, right then and there on the marble steps of the White

House. Despite all the suffering by his loyal men, the carnage and bloodshed on both sides was aging him as fast as Lincoln. Historians and romanticists like to write about this handsome and dashing leader passing through towns on his gray charger, the Northern women wishing he fought for them.

And then: Dwayne let his pencil fall from his left hand; he heard it land and roll beneath him. His eyes went to the marble face looming below the scudding clouds in the October sky. It dawned on him: that he, also a simple man, who wrote fictitious stories today because he had no desire to be confined to the American office routine. That mind-set is what made him a rebel today and kept him clear of the herd. And he had always been like that, and that's why the fascination with Lee, the ultimate rebel. So what if he is related to the man? So are ten thousand others. There was no past life he could possibly be living today via that man of marble up there; there was nothing about Lee's daughter Annie to work through in The Wilderness. That was merely a writer's imagination, for R. E. Lee was not coming back because he had no lessons to learn today. He, like Lincoln, was here for the last time. They were tested beyond belief and passed with flying colors.

But I, as I sit here before Lee's marble face, I regress to the time my own brother called me a coward. He had never said that before, and it was one of the last times I saw him alive.

I had hurt his feelings earlier that day by telling him on the phone I was moving out of his place because he was a moron. He was losing projected real estate prospects he'd been nursing with tons of time and energy on the phone and running around Phoenix. Later that night when I arrived home at his condo we were sharing, he was seated at his desk in front of his blank computer screen on that wooden chair our mother gave him, his hairy back slouched forward from his burly shoulders. I know now, that my proud brother was carrying a lot of grief from the bad thoughts about his dream to be a big shot realtor—dying fast. I was two feet from him and stopped. Not a word from me. Those blazing blue eyes were on me. They were not the loving eyes of my brother I called Hoss; he had the Teddy Bear temperament of Bonanza's Hoss Cartwright. They were the big/round baby blue eyes of a man crazed beyond help, a bi-polar pair of blues I still see burning wide-eyed so close to me, saying angrily:

—What are you smilin' at?

I headed into my room and he followed me. I sat down on the end of my bed because I did not want to get physical with him and destroy me and my room. He stood a few feet in front of me telling me how when he was a boy I would pick on him, and that I was a coward then and now because I wouldn't fight him man to man. I got out of my room and near his desk when he pushed me. I hurt my elbow on the wall from the force of his push. He went outside, calling me out; I went to the doorway, saw him standing there stiff-legged with his fists clenched ready to pulverize me. I closed the door and considered locking it, but instead, went into my room locking the door. I told him to go away. He played his country/western music loud all night 'til four in the morning.

What's so haunting: I had the chance to let myself and my brother confront our past and let him release his grief and anger that was bottled up inside. Love wasn't there between us at all. I could've asked for forgiveness. Yes, proud brother, I was the coward because I did nothing. I know now I could have begun to heal the pain between us and perhaps let us see that more of this letting go was needed to destroy the evil bitterness between brothers.

Though half-brothers in blood, sharing the same womb made us whole brothers who entered this world from the same place yet eight years apart.

Dwayne was never really satisfied with the words he wrote, or attempted to say, for he could never express in words what it felt like to lose his brother, his best friend.

Again, into the face of the man in marble, this man who would rather die a thousand deaths than surrender. This man of long ago who was much like my own brother, who also finally surrendered, gave up, but to that unknown void after darkness: death.

He walked down a long residential street lined with tall oaks and cottonwoods away from his ride in the same direction of the marble Traveller that soon turned to lavish antebellum homes. The names on the bronze historical markers on the homes were those of doctors, merchants, traders, and politicians, all Southern officers and gentlemen of Richmond, their homes preserved by the Daughters of the Confederacy.

A turn west onto Franklin Street and there before him stood at 807 Franklin, a white two-story Victorian house with forest green trim. The marker said: "The Clayton House," circa 1839, Lieutenant Jeb G. Clayton, C.S.A. Then, as at Wolfe's Dixieland, his eyes scanned for a way in, though he was not certain if the house was occupied, vacant, or open for touring.

From Something Bad

During lunch William told Jerilyn he would move into the Sheraton tomorrow after he got his commission from her prize money. He was contrite about the way he had acted around that stranger.

She wanted to talk about her dreams and the past life connection she felt with the stranger. But William was in no mood to hear about that nonsense. She noticed that his arm seemed to bother him more when she talked about such things.

But money changes such things. William's spirit was high; he laughed often during lunch. Jerilyn was in love with his laugh, so deep and loud; and he laughed more when she said she'd give him cash tomorrow.

During one of his big laughs, Jerilyn's cell phone rang. It was the stranger. William pretended he wasn't curious who it was, but from her silence during the call he couldn't help notice her writing down 807 Franklin in her planner. He could see her eyes expressing deception. After she clicked off and returned her phone to her purse, he excused himself and called the Sheraton from a pay phone. He didn't want to see that awkward time when she felt obligated to tell him that stranger just called her. He knew.

Later that night: Jerilyn's reading Dwayne's book in bed. After she turns a page her concentration moves to her open planner on her nightstand, to "The Clayton House" and 807 Franklin Street.

Ms. Virginia gets out of bed and puts on a pair of gray jogging pants and sweatshirt.

Chris Rea's song *I Can Hear Your Heartbeat* begins as Jerilyn comes running out of her apartment building, jogging down he lit sidewalk in running shoes. She runs past several Victorian omes as:

William's relaxing on a king-sized bed in his new room watching a movie when he has the urge to call Jerilyn, dialing his bedside phone. No answer.

The song continues as Jerilyn reaches Franklin Street. Soon he sees 807 Franklin on The Clayton House. There's only a lone ght shining on the small porch. No lights are on inside the house. As she slowly ascends the front steps, the music fades out after she urns the front door handle and it opens.

When he heard the door creak open downstairs, he really hought it was the door to his true soul, the same door Thomas Wolfe wrote about with such intensity. Dwayne remained quiet. She must come to him. At first, he worried that she might leave upon seeing the furniture blanketed with clear plastic. Yet she could see nothing; she was guided by a past familiarness she knew well as he lay on the small cot with a throbbing headache in the servants' room at the end of the hall upstairs, with the door closed purposely because he saw so clearly that it had to be closed as it was so long ago. And that she had to come to him, just like little osie came to Floyd in his novel *The Paper Man*.

Shots of adrenalin were making his feet perspire until he saw a flash, then a brilliant gold light as the room spun until he was unconscious. He could see he was leaving the room like a specter might, as:

Again, William is concerned after dialing Jerilyn's number with no answer as:

Jerilyn reached the top of the dark stairway. Her heart was racing like when a little girl and often afraid of the dark. Her trembling hands were raised slightly as she walked instinctively toward the open door of the servants' room where Dwayne had left just moments ago.

She entered the dark room and lit a candle on an unfinished bedside table of pine at the head of the narrow canvas cot. She knew that there was no mirror in the tiny sleeping room, but went over to a wooden crate with no lid and took out a stiff burlap / cotton nightgown and held it to her face, smelling it, knowing it was fabric from another time. She carried it over to the window with the candle and could see her reflection. Her skin was darker and rough to her touch; she was younger, perhaps eighteen. Her eyes were a darker liquid brown. She touched each breast as they were smaller than those of Jerilyn.

After returning the burning candle in the bronze holder to the small table by the cot, she undressed slowly, consumed with these physical changes that were not hers but moments ago. Then, naked, she went back to her reflection in the window without the candle. Upon seeing her slender figure she touched her coarse black triangle of hair that was much thicker than Jerilyn's. She moved her hand to her legs and could feel the unshaven legs of a servant girl.

This time: her eyes looked through the glass. It was deep into summer in 1864; there were no streetlights burning or lights from other homes on the street. She could see an old chestnut colored horse lazily standing in front of a buggy it was hitched to across the road, a dirt road. There was no fear coming from who she was now as she left her candle burning at the head of the cot and curled up under a muslin blanket listening for someone as:

Inside Jerilyn's apartment building, William winces from pain as his left arm is killing him when unlocking Jerilyn's apartment door with a key. Before closing the door behind him he calls her name. No answer. He goes into her bedroom and picks up her day planner that's open to the address of The Clayton

House.

Moments earlier, the four-poster bed in the master bedroom had been draped with a clear plastic cover. When Dwayne turned away from the dormer window, he was wearing the soiled Confederate uniform of a lieutenant, his hat in hand. He went over to a mirror and saw the reflection of a stranger with curly brown hair, a full beard and was at least three inches shorter. Before turning to bed he thought: Is this how I'm related to Marse Robert?

Then: on the far side of the bed, he could see the sleeping figure of a frail woman under the covers. Beside her, close to the bed, a cumbersome wooden wheelchair is parked. He remembered that Lee's wife was an invalid unable to walk. He left the room quietly, his wife snoring like a longshoreman.

Lieutenant Clayton entered his servants' room. He opened the lone window, for it was late July and awfully hot with no breeze. This wasn't the first time he whispered to her while standing over her cot as she pretended to be asleep:

—Shy Ann.

He beheld those great protruding eyes that were like wet black grapes in this dark stifling cubbyhole; they were eyes more scared than the times before, because part of her wanted him. She could hear him undress in the dark. His uniform and body had the familiar smells of war: old sweat, gun powder, dust, and dried mud mixed with the lathered odors of horse and mule.

She sighed a whispered protest as he took her fast without intimacy. Then, when he was done she turned away curled to the wall. As he dressed, he heard her quiet sobbing. When dressed, he sat on her cot and turned her face gently in order to see her, and whispered:

—Shy Ann, you must know I don't do this to hurt you. I'm still a young man...my wife is unable to be with me.

There was nothing discernable except shame in her dark eyes; this was the only man she had been with. She liked Mrs. Clayton and thought of them kindly as a couple; they were good to her.

Then: when she felt his weight shift as if leaving, this servant girl who barely uttered a word during each day:

—I don't like you to come to my bed, Mr. Clayton. It's a bad thing for sure, she whispered.

She turned away from his eyes, back to the wall with one of her hands fisted in front of her trembling mouth with barely a breath left in her lungs.

He left her without another word, knowing he could not promise he would not take her, for he'd done that many times while in the field. He knew the only way he could promise her such a thing is if he were killed in action. For Shy Ann, this taciturn servant girl whom his wife taught to read and write, was the only physical thing he had to look forward to. Just when he bent down and touched her trembling shoulder:

They turned back into Jerilyn and Dwayne, dressed in their clothes, both aware of what had just happened. Jerilyn's brown eyes seared into his pale blue eyes that were now aglow as if fully alive. They remained quiet, breathing together; she still felt as if she had just been with him. The awful brutality of what he had done to her did not anger her, for she knew right then and there a big part of her heritage. No anger.

Dwayne was now smiling, to let her know he would not harm her, and, that it was not really he who just took her body with such callousness. Jerilyn sat up on the cot; she straightened her sweatshirt sleeves and looked down to the floor in the candlelit room as if ashamed of what happened.

—What's going on? he whispered, wanting her to look at him.

She kept her head down, nodding many times before answering:

—I don't know. It's all so strange.

hen, he sat next to her and grabbed her shoulders as he did outside
er father's church and turned her to him, anxious to know what
ad just happened. When she looked at him and held his gaze, he
sked her calmly:

—Jerilyn, you do know. Your grandmother knows, doesn't
he?

he began to cry, unable to speak, as:

Outside The Clayton House, on the sidewalk, William was
fraid to go any further as he perspires heavily and can see the
andlelight's auburn glow coming from an upstairs window. He's
o fearful that if he goes one step more, something terrible will
appen. When he mustered enough courage to step forward, a
linding swirling cinnamon-colored light brought him to his knees
nd spun him counterclockwise to the ground, the same way
wayne was hit at Appomattox.

When he opened his eyes: he was perspiring even more
rom the summer heat. He had a rifle in hand waiting for the
xplosion from the dynamite tunneled under the Confederate lines
uring the siege at Petersburg. He was crouched in a trench
vearing the uniform of the Union blue. He knew nothing of
Villiam, as he had been waiting a protracted amount of time as a
ergeant about to lead his all-black company and take the Rebels by
urprise as they recovered from the blast.

He knew he was Sergeant Ellison from Baltimore and that
his was near the end of July in 1864.

Finally: a tremendous blast ripped out a 200-foot crater
hirty feet deep near the Confederate lines. Lieutenant Clayton and
is Rebel men are covered with dirt and dust. There's incredible
onfusion as Ellison's men are blinded from the cloud of debris
hat's everywhere.

—FIX BAYONETS! Ellison orders his men. STAY LOW!

Lieutenant Clayton is in awe of the deep crater, but is surprised that the enemy has not advanced as Rebel troops arrive on the crater's rim as:

Sergeant Ellison is waiting for a signal to advance. To himself:

—Come on! We can't wait here!

Ellison's troops are poised for the assault and look to their sergeant to explain the delay. Ellison motions for his men to remain calm and wait for orders, then:

William comes out of his past life flashback; he's sweating profusely while curled up in the fetal position on the sidewalk in front of The Clayton House. Then, he gets to his feet, looks around and checks his clothing before walking toward the house.

He pushes open the front door quietly. In The Clayton House entryway William's breathing hard; he's frightened when he stands at the bottom of the staircase and shuddering while looking upstairs. Then: just as he takes the first step: Past Life Flashback:

Ellison's men are restless from the delay to advance after the explosion. A Union officer hustles over to Ellison in the trench. He salutes the white officer, which the officer returns:

—Sergeant, advance your men.

—But, sir, it's been too long! They's ready for us by now!

—You have your orders, Sergeant.

—Yes, sir. Prepare to advance! Ellison calls out to the faces of his men down the line. FORWARD!

Union artillery fire covers Ellison's men during the assault as Ellison and his men climb out of their breastworks and run uphill with fixed bayonets toward the crater. We follow Ellison's footsteps until: END OF FLASHBACK.

At the bottom of The Clayton House staircase, William's legs are weak, he's breathing and perspiring heavily as he slowly oves upstairs, his left arm hurting as it did at the auditorium. He reads reaching the top of the stairs, shaking his head back and orth as if not wanting to see what's coming: PAST LIFE FLASH-ACK:

As Ellison and his men arrive at the edge of the huge crater s men rush into the hole as Ellison stands on the crater's edge oking for the enemy. While waves of his excited men fill the ater, Ellison senses a trap, but it's too late.

Rebels raise up and fire down into the crater, slaughtering llison's men. Rebel shouts of obscenities: NO NIGGERS AKEN ALIVE!

Ellison fires his pistol at Rebels while reaching down into e crater with his left arm, trying to pull out one of his trapped en. Just then: Ellison is shot below his left shoulder; he falls ounded into the dark pit on top of his trapped men. Lieutenant layton is appalled at the Yankee carnage in the crater. He orders s men to cease fire yet enraged Rebels continue firing into the led heap of wounded and dead Yankees. Finally, the firing stops. Rebel commander surveys the crater near Clayton.

—Colonel, request permission to remove the enemy's ounded.

—I'll hang any man who aids those vermin. he colonel leaves Clayton stunned. END OF FLASHBACK.

Dwayne and Jerilyn are still sitting on the cot in the ervants' room where they hear someone fall hard down the aircase. They cautiously descend the stairs until they see that Villiam is unconscious at the bottom of the stairs.

—It's William! Call 911! Jerilyn screams.

—No! He has to go through this! Help me get him pstairs!

—No! The basement, Jerilyn insists.

They look in the direction of the closed door that leads to the basement, then together manage to drag William's limp body to the top of the basement stairs whereupon: PAST LIFE FLASHBACK:

Lieutenant Clayton carries a lit lantern into the crater with two of his tattered men. Moaning comes from the pile of dead black Union soldiers. Clayton shines his lamp on Ellison's tortured face:
—Get this man out.
The Rebels move Union dead until they free Ellison. Clayton pours water from his canteen onto Ellison's face then gives him a drink:
—Easy...easy.
Clayton shines his lamp on Ellison's wound and orders the men to get him out and to be careful of his wound. Ellison looks for his men while being carried out of the crater:
—My men...help them.
Clayton covers Ellison's mouth, telling him to be still.

They put the wounded Ellison into the back of a wagon pulled by a mule. Before Clayton covers Ellison's upper body with a blanket he tells the wounded man to keep covered. Clayton drives the wagon alone away from the sleeping Rebel lines.

At dawn Clayton drives the wagon through Richmond's cobblestone streets until he stops in front of a large home. He uncovers Ellison's feverish face and tells him after giving him some water:
—I'm after a doctor to look at you.
He covers Ellison again and hurries to the front door of the doctor's house.

Clayton pounds on the front door until a groggy-eyed Doctor Blum, a middle-aged Jewish man opens his door:
—Doctor Blum, I'm sorry for this intrusion, but I have a wounded man who needs your help at once.

The doctor stepped outside putting on his glasses while

walking over to the wagon. When Blum uncovers Ellison he's shocked when he sees a black Union soldier. After covering him:

—Why'd you bring him here?

The doctor starts to walk away:

—Doc...please.

The doctor stops and turns back to Clayton:

—If I treat him they'll hang me.

—Doc, if you don't treat him he'll die. I'll take responsibility.

The doctor heads for his house, saying:

—I've got a family to think about.

—So does he.

Turning back to Clayton, he says:

—Not here.

Shy Ann sees the lieutenant at dawn from a window helping Ellison out of the wagon. She hurries away.

Downstairs Shy Ann helps Clayton carry the semi-conscious sergeant down the basement stairs. He tells Shy Ann to clear the table. Shy Ann hurriedly clears the wash table, then helps Clayton put the wounded man gently on the table. Clayton lights a lantern as she inspects his wound:

—He has to have a doctor.

—Doc Blum is coming. Boil some water and bring me a bottle of whiskey from the cabinet. Is my wife home?

—No, sir...she's gone to find some sugar beets from a peddler.

—Help me get his shirt off.

Ellison moans as they remove his blood-soaked blue coat, ranting about his men and that he has to get back to them.

—Your men have been taken care of. Stay still.

Just then: the doctor arrived with his medical bag; he tells Ellison:

—the doctor's here to look at your arm.

Blum examines Ellison's wound as Clayton holds the lantern. Blum tells them he'll need boiled water, whiskey and fresh linen. Shy Ann hurries away as Blum rolls up his sleeves. Blum tells Ellison:

   —Your arm's shattered. If I don't take it off, you'll die.

Ellison's fearful eyes close as Shy Ann hands the doctor the bottle of whiskey. Blum tells the sergeant to get as drunk as he can. To Shy Ann:

   —Pour that bottle into him.

As she pours whiskey into Ellison, Blum rolls up his sleeves and removes a cutting saw from his bag as Clayton heads upstairs to get boiled water.

   Ellison's eyes are glazed from pain and liquor as Shy Ann continues pouring whiskey into him.

   —My ring...

She looks down to his left hand and removes a man's gold wedding band from his little finger. He lifts his right hand for her to slip it on. After she puts the ring on his right little finger, she continues pouring liquor into him. She becomes terrified when she sees the doctor sharpening his saw.

The patient sounds drunk:

   —It's my father's wedding band. It's for good luck, he laughs.

She continues pouring:

   —What's yer name? he smiles.

   —Shy Ann.

   —How do you spell it?

After she spells her name for him:

   —That's beautiful.

   —Thank you.

   —Well, Shy Ann, I'd ask ya to hold my hand...Ellison laughs loud, referring to his left hand, soon to be amputated. She's not amused. She stops pouring and pats his forehead with a wet cloth.

—Shy Ann, you ever see a Negro Yankee?

She nods no and pours more into him.

—I used to be property. No more of that. Now I's the property of Mister Lincoln. He's gonna free us all...if Grant don't kill us first.

Ellison laughs until Clayton returns with a kettle of boiled water. The doctor appears ready to use his saw. Ellison grabs the whiskey bottle from Shy Ann with his right hand, then takes a long drink from the bottle. Blum looks into his patient's eyes before he places a piece of wood between Ellison's teeth:

—I have no morphine.

Blum and Clayton quickly tie Ellison's legs and right arm to the table as Shy Ann pours more whiskey into him. Blum tells Clayton to hold his shoulders to the table. Clayton stands above Ellison's head, with a grip on each shoulder. Ellison bites down hard on the wood in searing pain as Blum pours alcohol on his wound. Shy Ann squeezes his right hand that wears the ring. Ellison closes his eyes as the doctor raises his saw to his patient's left shoulder. The pain on Ellison's face is excruciating when Blum saws into bone as Clayton struggles to keep him pinned to the table. Shy Ann prays with her eyes closed. END OF FLASHBACK.

Dwayne and Jerilyn are exhausted after re-experiencing the amputation. Jerilyn's holding William's right hand, and Dwayne has released his grip on William's shoulder as William is passed out on the basement floor from trauma. Jerilyn calls his name:

—William.

William comes out of his ordeal looking down to his left arm to his hand, wiggling his fingers, and glad they are still there. He smiles at Jerilyn. And now William's eyes are on Dwayne like a brother, a brother who saved his life.

Dwayne wants to tell this man about his brother, and how he didn't or couldn't save him; and he wants to know how he can save a stranger in a past life and lose his brother in this one. Then, he realized he may have had a life or two between Lieutenant Clayton and Dwayne Dayne. Right now, he didn't really want to know about anymore past lives he may have had.

William is still too enervated to get up from the floor as he looks around the basement:

—Whew...that was too much. How'd I get down here?

—We carried you, Jerilyn said.

—Who are you? William asked Dwayne.

—Dwayne Dayne. Don't laugh.

—Dwayne Dayne? You were a Rebel officer?

He nods yes.

—You saved my life.

Dwayne smiles at William as Jerilyn holds his hand. She's excited when William exclaims:

—All of us...we were...there?

Dwayne and Jerilyn nod yes. William tells Dwayne:

—That's why I felt strange around you.

Dwayne nods and asks:

—How do you feel now? How's your arm?

William reflects on how he feels while flexing and moving his left arm:

—I feel...joyous...not like me. My arm's fine.

Jerilyn bends down embracing William as he cries tears of joy, blubbering:

—I feel...joy. I don't remember the last time I felt this way.

Now William sees Dwayne as a great friend, extending his arm up for Dwayne to join in hugging with Jerilyn. All three embrace, laughing tears of joy as William tells them:

—That was no dream. I could feel my arm leaving me. Oh, God...it really happened. One thing: before I fell down the stairs...what were you two doing?

Jerilyn and Dwayne look at each other, then burst out laughing.

William laughs, too, not sure why. Dwayne tells him that they were waiting for him.

Later: in The Clayton House master bedroom, a candle burns on the bedside table as Jerilyn lies on the bed between William and Dwayne. All breathe deeply with their eyes closed while holding hands. Dwayne puts his free hand, palm up, on Jerilyn's stomach, telling William to take his hand, then: PAST LIFE FLASHBACK:

In The Clayton House bedroom at night, Mrs. Clayton, in her wheelchair, pours the recovering Ellison a drink of water while he lies in bed with a high fever. Jerilyn is concerned about his delirious moaning for his men. Mrs. Clayton, in her Southern accent, asks her house servant:

—Did my husband leave a note for me?

Nervously, Shy Ann replies:

—No, Mrs. Clayton...no note, ma'am. Mr. Clayton said he had to get back soon or catch trouble.

Just then: Shy Ann nearly faints. Mrs. Clayton follows her in her wheelchair into Shy Ann's room across the hall.

Shy Ann's holding her stomach while lying on her bed. She does not want eye contact with Mrs. Clayton when the crippled woman tells her:

—You've never lied to me, Shy Ann. I'm not a stupid woman. I know you are pregnant.

Mary gently turns Shy Ann's face to her:

—I'd say you were some four months along. So...your baby was conceived about the time I went to Lynchburg.

Shy Ann's contrite face listens:

—So, that's why he brought this Negro Yankee into our home. Isn't my husband a thoughtful man?

Her servant is scared, as Mrs. Clayton sighs, resigned to the truth, patting Shy Ann's arm:

—Rest. I'll look after the sergeant.
Shy Ann cries after Mrs. Clayton wheels out of the room. END OF
FLASHBACK.

They wake up together with Jerilyn still holding a hand of
each man on her belly. William did not want to see anymore, but
Jerilyn and Dwayne do. Jerilyn's been crying as William helps her
up and off the bed:
—You okay, baby?
She nods yes.   William extends his right hand to handshake with
the writer, saying, as they shook:
—Thanks, man. Whatever the reason, you saved my life.
So, you two were lovers in a past life? They say nothing, then,
William starts to usher Jerilyn out of the room, and Dwayne tells
them that they have to come back tonight. William answers:
—Look, we have some big commitments up north.
—Cancel them. We have to see more.
—He's right, she agrees.
—We can't miss this photo shoot. They'll sue both of us.
William knows Dwayne is right. Jerilyn adds:
—If we see this through...we'll be able to do anything we
want.
William gives in.
—I'll make some calls. What time should we met you here?

That morning, Jerilyn and William hold hands while seated
in front of a banker's desk. The banker returns, handing Jerilyn a
receipt:
—Ms. Haynes...or should I say...Ms. Virginia. And
William...here's your deposit slip receipt for ninety thousand in
Jerilyn's account and ten thousand in your account...minus this five
hundred in cash.
Outside the bank, William's elated to have some money in

is pocket as he walks Jerilyn to work:

—Babe, since you're only workin' a half day today and it's our last day, take the morning off and come play with me.

—I can't. I have to train that new guide before I go.

—Okay, I'll push up that Vogue shoot and close that car commercial.

—Just make sure it's not a used car commercial.

They laugh; then William says:

—Remember that guy who wanted you to drive that used Caddy in his commercial? You said you ain't drivin' no cracker through Richmond!

They laugh until they reached the Confederate Museum. Then William gets serious:

—Yeah, that was somethin' out of this world last night. One of the reasons I even agreed to go back to that place is maybe you'll stop having those dreams and we can move on.

Jerilyn puts her arms around William and hugs him as he says:

—I want you dreamin' about me.

She laughs and kisses him, then she rubs his arm:

—How's your arm?

—Fine. Baby, that's what's so amazing.

—I know. I gotta go.

—Pick ya up for lunch?

—I'll call ya and let ya know then. You gonna be in your room?

—Yeah.

William watches Jerilyn walk into the museum before walking away as:

From Traveller: Dwayne watches William walk away.

Jerilyn's surprised when she sees Dwayne enter the drafty museum:

—What are you doing here?

-213-

—I have to know for sure what happened back then. Meet me at The Clayton House earlier, before William gets there.

—I can't go without telling him.

—We won't find out with William there. It's too painful for him. He won't see what he doesn't want to see.

Jerilyn's thinking it over as her replacement waits for her:

—I have to go. How do you get in there?

—Meet me there at eight.

From William's POV he sees Dwayne exit the museum.

Later: at lunch, William and Jerilyn share a quiet table. He toasts:

—So...your tour guide days are over. To Ms. Virginia.

After toasting, he asks here what time they are to be at The Clayton House:

—Midnight.

—Why can't we meet there at nine or ten...why so late?

She shrugs her shoulders; she's bothered because of planning to secretly meet Dwayne early:

—You seem quiet, babe. Everything okay with you?

—Uh huh...I'm fine. I guess I'm just anxious to get this over with.

William nods in agreement, adding:

—This past life stuff is wearin' me out. Why don't we go back to my place...and relax? We don't have to go through that again.

—No, we have to do this. I just wanna go home, finish packing and be alone tonight.

William pretends to understand, placing his hand tenderly on her hand and telling her that he'll pick her up at 11:30.

It was near 8:00 P.M. when Jerilyn reached The Clayton

House and found Dwayne pacing the sidewalk in front of the house:

—We can't get in. The window I used is locked now. I saw a patrol car cruising by when I got here. A neighbor must've seen us here.

—It's just as well. I don't like doing this without William.

—There's only one other place we can go.

Traveller is parked near the Petersburg crater. As they walk:

—You anxious to be Ms. Virginia?

—Ya know, I'm not so sure anymore. It doesn't seem as important. I was thinking about it in church. Is this for me or my parents?

—...or William?

—It was about color. There's a big part of America that's white, corporate, and ugly. These same people wouldn't stop to say hi to me on the street if I wasn't selling their product. That's just the way it is. And I was willing to put up with it...to make it. Now...I don't know.

They reached the spot where Lieutenant Clayton rescued Sergeant Ellison. Floodlights shine down into the wide and deep crater as they stand at the crater's edge:

—This is where Sergeant Ellison's men were slaughtered and he was wounded.

—Why would they go in there? Jerilyn asked.
Jerilyn is shocked to see William approaching them; he's sweating and terrified. Dwayne knew William had been following them, since he saw William waiting in his car near The Clayton House.
He knew that this was the only way to get William to come here.

—William! Jerilyn cries.
William's angry and sobbing while standing still, unable to move.
To Dwayne:

—Why couldn't you let me die with my men?

—William, you're almost through this.

William's knees buckle when he steps toward Dwayne. Then, he struggles to his feet and lunges for Dwayne, knocking him to the ground. Dwayne motions for Jerilyn to stay away and asks William:

—Why'd you come here?

William, terrified, his head nodding no as he crawls away from Dwayne. They roll and wrestle on the cold ground; William's overpowering Dwayne as Jerilyn watches helplessly. Dwayne tells her to pin one of his arms. Just when Jerilyn easily pins his left arm, William lets out this agonal scream that appears to calm him. Dwayne tells him, as they both keep him pressed to the earth:

—We've gotta go back, William!

William begins to sob, terrified of his past life as Jerilyn comforts him by stroking his eyes shut:

—I'll stay with ya, baby.

—Hold his hand.

All three lie on their backs with each holding one of William's hands. At first: nothing. Then: the trio's breathing is labored as they spin around and around in a brown mist, until: PAST LIFE FLASHBACK:

Back to that summer night in 1864 after the massacre in the crater. It was right after Ellison's amputation, Lieutenant Clayton returns from Richmond with the wagon. He looks down into the crater covering his nose from the stench. Dead black Union soldiers are still heaped in terrible carnage. A rifle shot is fired into one of the dead from a hidden Rebel.

The same Confederate colonel is chatting with a Rebel sergeant and junior officer when Clayton bursts into the colonel's tent:

—Colonel, why haven't those men been removed from that pit?

—Are you suggesting, Lieutenant, that we take care of those men?

—A Union burial detail must have petitioned you, sir.
The colonel's eyes go to the sergeant and junior officer to get their patented answers. Both men nod no and make light of it with their manner.

—Apparently, the enemy has no concern for those...men, the colonel grinned.

—Colonel, I beg you to summon a Union burial detail! Our men are firing rounds into their dead bodies! Or...I will appeal to General Lee.

—Lieutenant, you are being jailed for leaving your post. Sergeant! Take his pistol and arrest this man.

In an upstairs Clayton House bedroom, the recovering Ellison opens his eyes when Shy Ann draws the curtains open, then checks his forehead for a fever.

—You're feelin' better.
She goes over to a window and opens it for fresh air; Ellison turns away, brooding over the loss of his arm.

—Would you like somethin' to eat?
No answer. She stands over, him asking him if he feels pain. Again, nothing.

—You don't have to talk to me. I understand.
Ellison turns to her in an angry whisper:

—House Nigger...you don't understand. What do you do...spend the rest of yer life waitin' on yer masters?! What's a one-armed Nigger gonna do?

—You be twice as busy, she smiles.
He fought his smile, then, out came his big laugh. She laughs with him as she pours him a glass of water, then she says:

—The way I see it...you gotta bunch to be thankful for.

—Any man who hires me, he be lookin' all day to see if I'm

keepin up, Ellison laughs, taking his glass of water.

     —Just keep that good feelin' inside.

After a drink, he needs help coping:

     —Tell me, Shy Ann, just how do you keep that good feelin'?

     —If I hum good thoughts to myself...soon...they go to my heart.

     —Who taught you to talk so right?

     —Mrs. Clayton. She taught me to read and write.

She's embarrassed when he asks here where she got her sweet spirit.

     —What good thoughts would you hum for me? he smiles.

She's amused and embarrassed as she thinks about it. Soon, she hums a beautiful tune for her patient. He's touched, and asks her to sing the words to him. Shy Ann lightly touches the ring on his right hand and sings softly while her fingers touch the ring:

Wounded soldier,

he can sing,

he's still here,

to wear this ring.

Together they sing the words until Mrs. Clayton calls for Shy Ann from her wheelchair downstairs:

     —Soldiers are here! Get him into the attic at once!

Shy Ann helps him out of bed and up to the attic.

     When Shy Ann found out that Mr. Clayton was sent to Libby Prison, she told William that Clayton is the father of her child.

     Ellison went with Shy Ann to help save Clayton's life. They ended up in the middle of the dirt road south of Petersburg that led to the armory across the river from Libby.

     It was here that General Lee passed with his staff on horseback and heard the tale of one of his lieutenants from a house servant and her one-armed husband. Marse Robert had Clayton released. Shy Ann and Ellison ran away to be married in Baltimore.

When the mist cleared, I was behind the wheel in Traveller near Baltimore, headed north. There was no Jerilyn or William when I awoke at the crater. They were characters I created a long time ago when I wrote a screenplay titled "Ms. Virginia." I had to see if my imagination could hold my story after saying goodbye to Ann in Fredericksburg. That is up to my readers.

As I neared the New York state line, I knew this was real. I was going to a place in my country where I could sell books like gangbusters. I hope.

Grey

I was afraid of going to this town where I was a celebrity. To have all eyes on me, for whatever reason, scared the hell outta me every mile closer to this town in Maine called Grey.

I tried to focus on the little towns I knew so well. I knew these towns as an outsider; I knew how much money they spent on things sold by a salesman; and, I knew the people would be friendly—as most were. Somehow, I knew that all would work out well in Grey, but my problem with Grey was—my writing was slipping. Sister Karen and her sidereal library stops that made me write about William and Jerilyn, and God knows what others ahead, was turning my writing into self-indulgent tripe.

It's hard for me to live when I'm writing. I get lost. And the red-hot core of the cruelest thing is still there. My brother wanted to sell my books with me. I turned him down when he said he could find me one good reader who could put me into the loop of published writers, a writer/in.

Now, he's dead. And the reader who could lead me into the loop was one dead old woman, who, in death, has given me hope. This hope gave me a plan to stop in Portland at a TV station, and let them know about my one good reader, and how this might interest their viewers.

Some forty miles from the Maine border, this cyclonic inspiration to write hit me. I pulled over on the shoulder and wrote this scene down, not having a clue why. I never know where my writing is going. It's the surprise I've managed to maintain over jaded hopes and things I want to happen while I'm angry at a God who would allow my brother to do such a horribly cruel thing to himself and my mother. I know it was all related to my brother and my father, the closest people I've lost in this life. Their deaths were forcing me to change. The scene:

I was on the beach in San Diego. An Asian man and his little daughter went into the water to play. He was so caring and attentive; he would pat the cold Pacific water onto her bare skin to get her body prepared for the icy water ahead. He held her hand along every inch of her journey into play. He was totally there for her. Totally.

I know I was not there for my brother and sister the way that man was. I did not want to be there at all for some seven thousand days and nights of fear and worry and shaken confidence. And now, it is against those seven thousand days and nights of abject uncertainty that I sit here unsure of tomorrow with my specious smile and aliveness that will fool only those like the Asian girl who was spared despair and aloneness in the coldest of waters.

The more he wrote, the angrier he became, until he broke the lead off his pencil. That's when he drove Traveller on, up 95 into the craggy rock territory of Maine, headed for Grey after he stops at the Portland News. He turned off the ringer to his cell phone, not wanting at all to hear from Karen and be distracted from going through with this public relations stop in Portland.

The air was charged with the sea and the crisp energy riding winds from Canada as the October sun shone just hot enough to bring sweat to his upper lip while marching uphill on Portland Avenue afer getting directions to the newspaper from a friendly pedestrian.

The faded jeans and orange sweater were snug against Dwayne's slight belly. Flash memories of other stops at Iowa and Nebraska newspapers when *Ledges* first came out were there so vivid, though he remained present in the moment and relaxed considering he was always aware that his writing was not quite good enough for bold moves like this. This kind of publicity about a deceased "one good reader" could catch a national audience. Just then: as he stepped down from the curb, another cyclone was coming. He stepped back up onto the sidewalk and focused on the present: he saw a brown garden spider curled dead, dangling from its web at the base of a corner mailbox; he saw a leashed blue merle Australian shepherd trot past the mailbox; the aroma of fresh-baked pastries caught him, their sweet fragrance had his eyes hunting for their location. Then: he was spinning again.

He dashed for the bakery's door, but stopped before going inside, for he did not want to squander this creative energy coming over him. Quickly, D. H. Dayne began writing upon reaching a bus bench twenty yards away. The last thought he had before he began writing: Everyplace Karen has sent me—this happens. This time I'm not gonna hug some tree. Just write and shut up.

I know now who or what Shy Ann is. She is my elusive fame, that shy lady who is terrified to come out and glow in her radiant sunshine. She is the woman side of me who controls my love, beauty, truth and passion, and anything creative I do.

She is not a black house servant from a past life, or a Dixieland tour guide, or Marse Robert's daughter. Without her cooperation, I'm but a hairy cipher with balls, designed mainly for hunting so I may feed my belly, and then drag my big belly and swollen balls over the high grasses where she hides from me. She hides from me because my present level of consciousness does not deserve her.

I wrote about her when I was a Midwest paper man, a toilet paper salesman traveling from town to town peddling my transparent 1-ply without mercy. Everybody was a prospect. I went to businesses, door to door. I became good at it. It freed me to write. Instead of becoming a drunk on a barstool, I was writing at a café booth or counter stool, writing feverishly at breakfast, lunch and dinner, at least ten thousand times.

One of the few times I did not write was the day I first met ny Shy Ann. I wrote this chapter about that day titled "She Held Me":

I am a young man now, and I don't understand how I got nto this business of being a paper man who sells toilet paper, paper owels and garbage bags in these hick towns and places that most people will never see.

I am a writer. I keep myself busy by thinking of stories that nterest me. This place is in the southeastern part of South Dakota, vhere there are treeless hills that keep you dry when spring floods :ome about every three years.

I was not far into a story that I thought had an interesting >eginning. My boss let me use his car when I sold. I parked it near a river that was swollen with spring rain and waited for a one-vehicle ferry that would shuttle me to an isolated Amish community :alled Doon. It was the only way to cross the river, though my 3outh Dakota readers will know there's not a ferry in the entire state today; but this was in 1974.

On this ferry: I was hunched over a picnic table holding a tin :up of weak coffee that warmed my hands. My sales case was against my side, hoping to soon hold an order from this large family of Mennonites that farmed a thousand acres and lived close ogether on three or four farms. The story was about this paper salesman who nearly dies when the ferry sinks.

He woke up in a queen-sized feather bed in a dark bedroom as the rain continued, wherever he was. He had been saved by three Amish girls, sisters, who lived with and cared for their elderly father in this old house that sat lopsided on a hill, surrounded now by water and mud and incessant rain.

The story was supposed to be about which world could pull the other in. Their world of candles, well water, baking with firewood, and curious potions to cure their father's illness, would clash with the paper man's dream to travel to faraway places, away from cornfields, mud, and animal shit.

The family were Mennonites from Holland; they were Anabaptists who baptized again in adulthood. The girls' rescue of the stranger was a good omen to them, as if he was baptized and cleansed of his sins and could be trusted to be in their home, a home that sanctioned polygamy and the literal sharing of everything.

The girls were worried about their father, who resembled a bloated Alfred Hitchcock with a long gray beard. Of course, the girls were all beautiful and I had to decide which one I liked the most. But my programming to be a monogamous American was foreign to their familial/communal upbringing. They shared everything, including me, without the "it's me or nothing" mentality that fuels the burgeoning miserable city populous. This wasn't "Misery."

One day, after being there for ten days of torturous flirting, and, with a giddiness I thought I'd lost when about ten years old, their beloved Papa died. I didn't know he died when I was sitting in the dark little kitchen at the table for four, having a cup of the best coffee I'd ever tasted, and a delicious rye bread that was baked in the same oven that warmed the house all day during the dreariest of rainy periods.

Sheila, the youngest, about 33, came into the kitchen and sat across from the salesman. Sheila's cheeks were swollen red; she'd been crying.

—Papa died, she whispered.

I don't know what came over me, but I felt safe for the first time that I could stop whispering, a habit the girls had from living with a martinet father.

—HE'S GONE! IT'S FREEDOM! I yelled.

This brought in the other girls to see what the commotion was about. Marian, 35, and Amy, the eldest at about 38, made it three pair of cornflower blue eyes with stupefied natural faces that had never known makeup; they were expecting me to wilt, apologize, shut down, anything but animate and roar my next words:

—YOU ARE FREE! YOUR PAPA IS FREE!

Only Amy the eldest sister wanted to hear more from this man from the outside world. The middle sister Marian went to their dead Papa's bedside and wailed for endless hours mourning her loss as the rain that pelted their gabled roof appeared that it would never end.

Amy listened to this toilet paper salesman's words about how he was not truly free to be a man until his father died. He pulled Amy outside by her hand where they were drenched by the rainwater. Soon, she became aware that she was washing away the years of stultification and denial that had put a deep furrow on her brow, a place that the paper man touched just before he kissed her.

As he kissed her, Sheila the youngest daughter saw this from her Papa's upstairs bedroom window. At first, she was appalled, then, she became jealous when she saw her ramrod sister run hand-in-hand with this outsider, before her Papa was even cold, into the barn, then closed the door behind them.

It was Amy who talked about Shy Ann, a term used by her Papa. Papa told his daughter that God had made women shy on purpose, in order to keep them pure, loyal, chaste until she took a husband.

When Dwayne came out of his writing trance, he was angry from thinking about a letter he received from a reader in Iowa who had read his three books placed in libraries, or, at least she had read some of them. This anger was what he had to feel in order to break away from his Shy Ann, his diffidence that kept him from being a writer/in. The walk to the Portland News was rife with the rebuff his Iowa reader gave him: "that he was not a REAL writer, a self-published one, and she went on to write that when she saw all the grammatical errors at the beginning of *Missouri Madness*, she was certain that if D. H. Dayne could get his work in print—she could.

The receptionist called the entertainment editor on her phone and told her that a writer was here to discuss an interesting story related to Maine and his writing.

Dwayne left the newspaper building confident the paper would send a reporter to his Grey book signing tomorrow evening. The editor thought it would make an upbeat story to close the 10 o'clock news.

He remembered the scene he wrote in the barn after the salesman was with Amy. She talked about how she had broken out of Shy Ann with him because her father was no longer around to punish her with guilt. This image of a God force ready to strike him down for seeking out publicity to promote his self-published work, stiffened his legs and slowed his walk, vacillating his body and mind over whether it was now good timing to get publicity for his writing. What if my work is no good? Now it will be publicized by the media, he worried. I make a good living as it is, he reminded himself. What if this ruins my book sales?

After turning a corner two blocks from the TV station, he mumbled Shy Ann while surveying the giant white clouds ahead. He knew he was terrified of success. He could handle being a struggling writer, but not authority telling him he had poor sentence structure and basic good grammar that's easy to read. Then he noticed that these clouds are moving easily and swiftly to the north in the direction of Grey.

His feet stopped on the Portland sidewalk. This was a new kind of October air rushing into his nostrils; it was air mixed with the sea, wet rock, and a palpable sense of timelessness. With eyes closed, he asked for a sign from Father Timing, God, Shy Ann... whatever. He could not handle media attention if they dismissed his work. He could handle a newspaper article, but cameras could ruin him if his work is not ready.

—Give me a sign. Please. Please.

He waited until a faith came over him that he will be shown a sign

—he continued walking—this sign he watched and listened for, and waited for, until he was conscious of a visceral sign that came from his belly that told him to go on. He continued on legs that pulled and flexed him closer to the station as if on licorice radar.

From his on-camera classes years ago, he knew he had to be positive and keep smiling, or he would come off as a dead-faced scoundrel looking for free publicity. He felt he was just that, he reasoned; why else would he be here?

Of course, the TV reporter that interviewed him was gorgeous, even though she wore makeup on every square inch of her face. Her name was Cheryl. After shaking hands he sat across from her desk. She listened:

—I'm an independent writer with four novels I published myself. I just came from the Portland News. They're going to be at my library book signing tomorrow night in Grey.
She smiled, knowing Grey.

—Anyway...the oldest resident and patron of the Grey Library was quite a reader. And, she died while reading my book. So, the whole town found out and now my books are popular there.

—How do you know she died while reading your book? Is that what caused her to die?

—No, of course not. She was found with my book open on her chest...in her reading chair. The librarian found this out from the lady's daughter. I call her my "one good reader"...that's a term I use to describe a reader who makes my books popular. So, the whole town wants my books. I don't know. I thought this might make a good story for your viewers.

He stood, ashamed of being so obvious about promoting his writing. That impressed her.

—Please sit down, Mr. Dayne, she smiled. I'm thinking of an angle here.

He sat on the edge of the chair ready to bolt if he picked up the slightest hint of chicanery, for he imagined being duped into appearing vainglorious, thus making all his critics and authors of his rejections right. That must never happen, he squirmed inwardly.

Cheryl leaned back in her castered high-back chair, touching the eraser end of her blue pencil to her glossy lips while thinking and looking past her guest. Suddenly, she sat up straight and leaned forward with her elbows on her desktop planner:

—We can get the lady's story from the librarian...and title the piece "One Good Reader" who just happened to pass away while in the throes of your book...and now...the book is a bestseller in this little town in Maine. "One Good Reader"...yeah...I like it. I'll run it by my producer. I have a good feeling about this. Can you be in the library an hour before the signing?

Grey was nothing like he imagined, yet, just as he imagined. He was allowed to park Traveller in the library parking lot. His walk to downtown Grey was underway when his first step left Traveller.

Main Street was a square or rows of businesses on each side of the street. Not in Grey. It was an angled wedge of three or four little shops off-shooting from the main highway that shot northeast into a lush forest of shade and curves. Grey was a disappointment to me. The most prosperous business was the Scotch Mart convenience store on the highway that rented videos and had a bakery that sold its residents delicious Maine potatoes for lunch.

Joann, the Grey librarian, was a stout woman in her 50's; she had a pretty face that had the stress of always needing money to buy books eleven out of every twelve months. She liked Dwayne right away, because his books were popular, and because he liked her. There was nothing new Joann revealed about his one good reader, besides her name and address.

Her name was Edna McConnell; she lived just three doors down from the library. After Joann told me we were standing in the small room that I was to have my signing in, I thought perhaps twenty people could sit here comfortably; and I could see that I didn't need a microphone. I told her that I would be an hour early because a reporter from Portland said she might show.

Before I left this library that was about twice the size of Traveller, she told me to go to the annual Grey Picnic tomorrow at 1:00 P.M., at the lake three blocks west of the library.

I stood on the sidewalk in front of Edna's little house that looked more like a cottage, with its faded yellow paint, white trim, and low flaky-white picket fence. I was thinking how I had no clue what I would say at the signing, and that was how I always wanted to live my life—on the fly. I was like Floyd in my novel *The Paper Man*, not wanting to clutter my head with things to remember. Just do it when I have to.

Then, I moved closer, all the way to the front room window and imagined where she was sitting reading my book *Ledges* in the now-empty house with the dull wood floor that gave me this dolorous thought with images: I could see my brother in a recliner all the way back, under a pole lamp, reading my book *Missouri Madness*, the story I dedicated to my brother, and I even used J. D., my brother's nickname, as the leading character. John never got to read the book; he was dead about the time it was finished. But I could see him there now with his big bald head and blazing blue eyes reading *Ledges* in one hand, then switching to *The Paper Man* that he held open in the other hand, back and forth from this story, then that story.

He read them both before he died. I held my image of my brother reading both books—all because he was reading them with an ulterior motive that made D. H. Dayne unwilling to tackle his diffidence, his Shy Ann. And it was so clear to me that dreams die if you do not keep them alive. Just then: my knees left me and I dropped to them while keeping the vision in this spin back some ten thousand days.

I could see that my brother had no more dreams and could

hardly sleep at all; he was so dead, already dead.

—Oh, God! Glorious blue-eyed brother...HOLD ON!
DON'T GO! DON'T LEAVE ME! YOU CAN HAVE MY
DREAM! I WILL GIVE YOU MY DREAM IF YOU COME
BACK TO ME! OH, GOD! HOW CAN YOU LET HIM PUT A
BULLET IN THAT HEAD I CARED FOR...AND KISSED
GOODNIGHT WHEN HE SLEPT...AS A BABY...A BOY...
WHEN HE WAS JOHNNY!!

Dwayne let the image go; however, his brain put words
across his conscience that fixed his eyes on Edna's reading spot.
His brother's words were begging him to let him sell his books door
to door to businesses; it was a product he just knew he could sell
and find his brother that "one good reader," and feel alive again. A
new dream.

—I turned him down, Dwayne whispered again and again
until he ordered himself to "STOP IT!"

Could this be his one good reader? he wondered, the same
reader he told his brother that he needed. The reader who would
truly "see" his stories, publish them, and soon—the film rights sold.
Did my brother kill himself because I rejected him? Was my turning
him away his last straw...his breaking point?

—STOP IT!!

I could see that Edna must've had a large collection of
knickknacks from the empty shelves lining most of the wall space.
I wondered what page she was on. And could an emotional scene
in *Ledges* have shut down Edna's heart? Could those moments of
heart wrenching pathos that gave *Ledges* its 300,000 readers been
her last emotion felt on this planet?

I looked at my watch. I was hungry and hadn't eaten all
day. The Scotch Mart sounded good compared to another meal
alone in Traveller.

As I ate some of the best fried chicken on the planet, I could
see and hear the town preparing for the picnic tomorrow:

—I'll bring the shoes and stakes, one customer told a clerk.

—I'll bring extra charcoal and T. J.'s bringin' the ice, the clerk returned.

It wasn't until the next day at the picnic that I found out why a picnic in October in Maine. M. K. Grey, founder of the town, was born on October 27th, so, the picnic named Grey Day is held on the last Saturday in October in Grey Park in a cozy rec room with a huge bonfire going in the granite fireplace in the middle of the large room.

It was really quite comfortable in there with all the windows open, circulating fresh air consumed by the blazing fire. Instead of sitting in the corner writing, avoiding conversation, I made it a point to let everybody know who I was, and if interested, please come to my signing later.

—Hi! My name is D. H. Dayne. I'm going to have a book signing in the Grey Library at eight tonight.

They all knew of my book *Ledges* and were very happy and excited to meet me. I could see in their eyes that they all knew that my book was the one Edna was reading when she croaked. They liked *Ledges*. Almost everyone talked about Gene the bus driver in the story and how much they liked him.

I took my dessert cup of rice pudding and found a place to sit off by myself near an open window that offered me a view of one of the most serene scenes I'd ever laid eyes on. Oval-shaped Lake Grey's azure blue water gave me insight about what I must do to be rid of this lack of confidence I called Shy Ann.

Real close to the window on a shelf, much like one of the shelves lining Edna McConnell's front room, my eyes studied this bunch of Kalanchoe standing in a dirty porcelain pot, bathing in the bright light it must have to survive. Its tiny orange petals, shaped like clover, had these yellow-green seeds deep in the center of each petal. I could see this incredible pattern of four petals and four seeds so alive in the sunshine that was hitting it perfectly, making this rich display of incredible orange color.

Then: I could really see my family, the four of them: my mother and sister; my brother and myself in these four petals that lived for this light, for this moment, or—they would die.

I thought I should write now or be overtaken by the cyclone, but I left Blacky in Traveller. Oh, God, I thought...I'll be on the floor in front of my readers, convulsing like a frigin' fish out of water. But I stayed on the Kalanchoe's brilliant orange petals and the lush green of the stems. There was no more use for imagined fear or the lack of anything in my life. In Asheville, I had resolved to change my life at Tom's grave. Then Ann the librarian found me. I did not run from her or my past. I cleared my debt to her and myself, and I held her body without taking it. That was a victory for me. In Richmond I saw my brother in William's eyes and was able to rescue him in my writing, though selfish ulterior motives were there. There was real proof now that I was unable, unwilling, or incapable of saving my brother in this life. Only in my writing, whether I'm escaping, hiding, or becoming a writer/ in—I must continue writing and learn to play along the way:

—It's time to play, I said to myself, over and over.

By chance, by accident, an old lady died reading my book. That may be as far as it goes, in Grey, Maine, this place where I'm known yet a stranger, a private world where all my books circulate because of one Edna McConnell.

Cheryl from Channel 12 didn't show until 7:30. Dwayne had been waiting since 6:30 with Joann the Grey librarian. There were two dozen folding chairs lined in four rows of six. When Cheryl came hustling into the tiny library with her cameraman, Dwayne had been sitting alone on a chair meditating for thirty minutes as if he was in Edgar Cayce's meditation garden. His ass was as numb as a Mexican cucumber. He had been quieting his ind in order to not think of things he would say; and, he had managed to let go the floodgates of worry inherited from his family.

Below Cheryl's clomping heels, Dwayne was as tranquil as baby with a big nipple. He was ready to play with her or any ther reporter that showed. Her usual control freak personality isappeared into his relaxed face. Automatically, he did nothing, efusing to rush away into the madness of action and words, and nages and lies.

He watched her shapely figure, then his eyes went up to her hort auburn hair, the color of hair he remembered seeing often on Kansas women. While she gave cogent orders to her obese ameraman and chatted quietly with Joann, Dwayne gladly left the resent to remember a time in Kansas when he was selling his nclaimed first novel *White Shoulders*, door to door to businesses. his was something he was going to use to fuel him during his nterview and book signing, a technique he'd learned in an acting lass in L. A.

It was summer in Liberal, Kansas in 1980. The main street vas torn up for construction, so no traffic could park. Dwayne, rmed with 500 copies of his first novel in the trunk of his black rans Am—attacked Liberal. He had the town to himself. And hey were his. Perfect timing.

As he sat there, oblivious to the Greyites filling seats behind im, and just when Cheryl was ready to interview him, he emembered that feeling in Liberal. He captured that essence in one antastic flash of memory that brought him to his feet; like John Candy in *Wayne*, his laugh was back, and a smile he hadn't seen on is dour mug since God knows when.

Cheryl was caught off guard. She saw his blue eyes flaring nd caught them meeting the eye of her camera lens to see if he was n. He knew where to look into the lens: through it, as if he were looking into a lover's eyes. Cheryl kept her camera on the writer as she stood beside him holding a mike:

—Mr. Dayne, the librarian tells me your books are quite popular here. And you are self-published...correct?

—Yes...thank God for my readers, he smiled at her, knowing to look at her.

—Why not get your books published the conventional way? Isn't this very difficult—selling your books to libraries yourself?

—Yes, but I do better than most writers because most writers aren't published. And, if it was easy...they'd all do it. That's why I do well...because it is hard. I love a challenge where I don't depend on anyone. I don't play golf...so, I sell books and come to book signings to meet my readers. I get to travel all over the country, find interesting things, places, and people to write about. It's all a dream, Cheryl.

Dwayne was relieved when Cheryl and company left the library. He went to the front of the room to a podium to face sixty of his readers crammed to the rafters; some he recognized from the picnic. The rush from being confident on camera, all from his image of Liberal, was staying with him. His voice was powerful, his face relaxed; and now he knew he must be that charming personality that sold ten thousand books, as the young writer from the Midwest who pitched to fifty thousand faces—one at a time.

He smiled until the rest of the room smiled back:

—Hi, Grey! Oh, don't worry about the TV camera...I'm not in trouble. They were here to find out about my books...and how in the world I could get so many readers in Grey...without a publisher. I was at the Grey Day picnic at the lake and talked to some of you. There's John and Beverly! Hi! Rob and Jeri! Hey! How many of you have read any of my books, or at least some of them?

All hands were raised.

—Wow! Let me say first...THANK YOU! Because of

you...I'm a writer. You, or most of you...tolerated my small print and poor sentence structure and grammar in *Ledges*. And you did the same with *The Paper Man*. *Missouri Madness* has helped my first two books circulate. Even though it's the worst thing I've ever written...it's the most popular. I only came here because of Edna McConnell. I didn't know her. But she knew me. She read some of *Ledges* or all of it...I don't know. I'm sure you all know that. Anyway, I went over to her house...

Dwayne's voice faltered. The audience was captivated yet uncomfortable when his hands trembled on the sides of the podium. He was fighting a cyclone that was trying to spin him down before his most prolific readers.

Most of them held their breath when they saw the amorphous of this stranger in their town whose face now turned round and bigger, and his hair appeared to vanish in a golden glow above his blazing blue eyes which were filled with the pain and anguish of his bi-polar brother. His head then shrank and it began this palsied negative nod of Gene the bus driver in *Ledges*; and just when his readers realized this was Gene Rainbow and this must be some kind of act: this calm came over this stranger. The ones who had read *The Paper Man* knew this was Harvey, the sensitive salesman and loner with whom Josie fell in love.

When all were breathing normally again, staying with him, trusting this stranger on this incredible emotional roller coaster ride, wherever it was taking them: the squeaky-hinged door to the library opened. The room turned and saw a beautiful brunette dressed in black jeans and flannel shirt. It was Ann Bruin the Asheville librarian and tour guide; Hope, the abandoned baby he used to help him sell his first novel. She stood in the doorway looking at the man whose face twitched around his eyes and mouth as his protagonist Leonard in *White Shoulders*. When he spoke, he stammered to the room while looking at her:

—This is Ann. She was abandoned at birth. She was found

by two boys skipping school...

She interrupted, stepping toward him:

—Dwayne, show them who you are. Those two boys who found me...they were Gene and D. J. in *Ledges*, weren't they, Dwayne?

He didn't answer; he stood at the podium as stiff as a carp, his ears ringing from those words. He wanted to speak; that trapped energy he always knew was stuck in his jaw...was ready to move. His breathing was labored now and his whole body on fire.

Ann pressed him, moving alongside the front row, urging him to break through to his true self:

—Keep going, Dwayne. Don't bail out. Show them who you are!

He began to cry; his face went ugly from the trapped anguish he'd been holding onto for so long. His eyes were flaring when he looked down, then up, unaware of his captivated audience when his head began that palsied negative nod, as if saying NO! NO! NO!, like Gene the bus driver in *Ledges*.

His readers recognized Gene. They listened as Gene was preparing to explode his words and bury them with his latent power as if they were the cruel antagonist Dutch in *Ledges*.

Forcefully from Ann:

—You are safe here, Dwayne. Show them who you are! Use your whole body! she demonstrated, raising her arms overhead.

To the room, he erupted with his entire being, his words coming from the deepest part of his belly, causing the nod to cease:

—I WAS GENE!! I WAS THE ONE WHO SURVIVED! D. J. WAS MY BROTHER!! HE COULDN'T LIVE WITH THE SHAME!!

—What shame? Ann pressed.

—OF BEING A FAILURE!! LOSING HIS DREAM!! AND I REJECTED HIM!!

—Why bring your crap here, Dwayne? These people don't
are about your problems. Tell them!
Dwayne's face is filled with rage, focused on Ann:
—Alright! I'll tell them! In my book Missouri Madness, I
vas struggling with Chief Linn's death. I couldn't find a way to kill
Albert or fake his death...to make everything fit.
—Tell them! she demanded.
To the room:
—I was worried about my brother. I was worried about my
mother worrying about my brother. I had to finish the story...for
the money...so I could sell it to my libraries. I forced the storyline
because of all of my family distractions. My brother called me. I
rejected him when he wanted to sell my books after his dream to
make it in real estate fell through. I didn't want his problems
around me when he begged me to let him come to Asheville to live
with me and sell my books. Because I was stuck on my plot in
Missouri Madness. I was obsessed with getting that bastard Kehoe
who killed all those people in Bath, Michigan in 1927! So...in a
way...he got my brother, too. He was calling me to save him! I
LET HIM GO!!
Softer:
—My brother shot himself a couple weeks later...the day I
finished the book. I miss him so much...and now...all I have is that
book dedicated to him...and my new one...*Shy Ann*. It's such a
cruel and terrible thing. I'm almost sold out of *Missouri Madness*.
There won't be anymore printed by me.
—Dwayne, you sound like a salesman now. Who was the
Paper Man?
—I WAS HARVEY! I WAS FLOYD! ME!!
—How are you like Harvey, Dwayne?
—I can sell you my books!
—What could Harvey do, Dwayne?
His breathing became faster and shorter with more emotion boiling

inside him. She repeated:

    —What could Harvey do, Dwayne?

    —Show you!

    —Show what, Dwayne?

    —HIS HEART!

    —And who was the King of Slugs, Dwayne, in *Missouri Madness*?

    —ME!!

    —Tell them why you wrote that stupid piece of shit, Dwayne!

    —I wrote about the biggest frigin' coward I could find!

    —Why, Dwayne?

    —Because I'm a coward!

    —Who said you're a coward, Dwayne?

    —My brother!

    —Why did he think you were a coward, Dwayne?

Dwayne swallowed hard; his memory was coming toward him like a Kansas tornado; another whirlwind was taking him down to his knees in anguish and tears as Ann stood over him and shouted for him to see it and to let it go.

Dwayne, now 16, can see the wall created by his own dysfunctional fears mirrored in the faces of his brother and sister. He was a bully to them, a coward trapped in fear and afraid to love. Then: he saw the fear begin to melt away from his siblings' smiling faces in ropes of orange and green electricity that ran out of his toes and fingertips. He was letting it all go, no longer willing to hold onto the fear, the unknown, the dead past he had inherited from so many generations.

    At that penultimate moment, on the floor of the Grey Library, D. H. Dayne let go of this genetic holding on that kept him lost and alone for most of his life. Ann and his readers watched in awe this transforming peace and calm taking over his entire body.

Ann knew that he had let go of a thousand things in these few minutes of raw courage he could only reveal to his readers.

When he got to his feet he could only laugh at his gape-jawed audience who had witnessed this transformation. He went over to Ann and pulled her body to his chest, hugging her while rocking back and forth while whispering "thank you" a dozen times at least. It was right then that he knew his powerful voice was back. He hadn't heard it in 20 years.

—How do I keep this? he whispered to Ann, still holding her.

—Tell them your dream and live it...every day.

—I want you to stay here for my book signing.

She smiled and found the floor comfortable against a wall off to Dwayne's side when he addressed the room with his true voice and aliveness:

—That was interesting! How many of you are writers?

Half the room raised a hand.

—I want to talk to you about your dreams. Your writing. Who cares about my books. Just read 'em...or don't. Tell me or ask me what you want to know about your writing, your dreams... anything!

A young lady in the back asked how he got his first book published.

—So, you would like to get your writing published?

—Yes.

—Are you willing to share your writing with the world?

—I think so.

—Your writing may not be ready to put out there, but you must be ready to take the rejection and criticism that will surely come if you self-publish. And if you try to market your own book...you'll quit and end up with five thousand copies in storage. How many of you are interested in self-publishing?

Some ten hands in the air.

—How many of you can sell five thousand copies?

No hands this time.

       —That's the only reason I'm here. Because I have the sales training and the ability to take rejection. I'm not here to discourage you, believe me. And I'm not here to give you a hot bath and raise your hopes about something I do. I guess...

He turned to Ann's smiling face looking up at him from the floor before he said:

       —I'm here to sell you my new book and tell you what a life of writing means to me, and how it can affect other lives in a positive way. I have to talk about me to reach you. I don't want to ramble on about my books or bore you with some passages. Lord knows I do that enough.

When he rolled his eyes and laughed at himself, the room laughed with and at him, for he had found his laugh again. It came from his belly and left his throat in an inchoate channel of sound health and aliveness. He continued...

       —I write from habit, in the morning, for a bit in a coffeehouse or café...away from where I live...because I work from home, marketing my books. I have to get out and write in places unrelated to my work space at home. That's changing a bit now that I live in a motor home and I'm on the road all the time. I've just started to live this way. I've done most of my writing at the end of my day after my phone work is done...in a restaurant after my evening meal. What I'm saying is be consistent. My body and mind are trained to write twice a day. And it just happens. I don't care if it's not worth a crap. All I care about is moving my story along. I may not use it. Sometimes I use it...and it's still no good. I have read where writers call good writing a craft and, after a good editor and validation by reviews from the publishing world, it's a work of art. Who decides that bunk? I say, any writing is a creation if you write for yourself from your heart...because nobody else writes like you do. A six-year-old child's letter to a mother...is so real and genuine...she will save it for a lifetime. That's art. The

hild did not know any elements of style or proper grammar or
vhere to place those commas and periods, or even correctly spell
alf the words. I'm like that child. I will tell my stories the way I
vant, the way I see 'em. I might use a dash instead of a comma;
nd teacher, I might misspell cue, and I certainly may run-on
entence my reader to the point of madness, to the point of
lamming my book shut with my name cursed all the way back to
he shelf. But, I will keep reading, wanting to improve. But please
lon't listen to that crap about craft if you've managed to somehow
it your ass down amidst all this organized chaos and madness in
ur media-driven reality to put your heart on paper. It's like the
ardest part of going to the gym to work out...is getting there. Any
uestions?

Later: after selling over a hundred copies of his new book,
e hugged Ann in the parking lot next to Traveller. She showed
im her new tires she bought with the money he gave her. She told
im she was driving back home to Portland and that she was going
o go back to school. He was headed west to his home state to a
unch of winter book signings in the Midwest. She said she would
ollow him until I-80 in Iowa, but she vanished again from his rear-
iew mirror after they passed the Maine state line. But he kept
lriving, unconcerned, for his mind was now ready to...begin again.

For orders and feedback:
Michael Frederick
P.O. Box 12487
LaJolla, CA 92039
(888) 810-1952
mfrederick310@aol.com

Michael Frederick is working on his 6th novel "Summer of '02" in LaJolla, CA.

"Shy Ann", 1st title in Michael Frederick's "WRITER series, is an experimental journey and must read for unpublished writer. D. H. Dayne's mission is to becc a recognized writer by following a sidereal travel ch created by his librarian sister, spinning her self-publis brother back into incredible past lives, mystery romance. All for the chance to live in the present become this writer/in.

ISBN 1-893794-03-2

90000

9 781893 794030

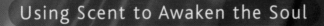

Using Scent to Awaken the Soul

The
Scented Veil

07 - CRL - 349

Carly Wall